IMMACULATE
CONCEPTION
CONVENT

Prayers,
Poems &
Songs

Prayers, Poems & Songs

Huub Oosterhuis

TRANSLATED BY DAVID SMITH

HERDER AND HERDER

1970
HERDER AND HERDER NEW YORK
232 Madison Avenue, New York 10016

Original edition:
In het voorbijgaan (first half),
Uitgeverij Ambo, Utrecht, The Netherlands.

Library of Congress Catalog Card Number: 76-122901
© 1970 by Herder and Herder, Inc.
Manufactured in the United States

Contents

Prayers, Poems & Songs

Two Poems

1.

Is it still allowed in church
to touch and feel in green or red,
sensing whether there is life
in making god with your hands from bread?

I am all for incense, like
to smell it near me if I can,
praying with my nose just as
a married woman prays to her man.

Like a child who slowly learns
to crawl and stand up, I too cling
to the practice once a week
of being close to the dead to sing.

2.

What I do so often
I long in tears to explain—
breaking bread and saying
strange things again and again.

Does it refer to something?
I hope so, but cannot state
that in those guilded secrets
man understands his own fate,

that bread means life, for instance
and life can also mean death.
Whatever I say, however,
that gospel is not in my breath.

Five Fragments About God

Then I sink into a chair
and think "God!" though I am not sure
which one of us I mean.

Leo Vroman

1.

In the middle of the seventeenth century, when Galileo for the first time saw the earth going round the sun, when the principles of modern science were discovered—to be more exact, on the night of the 23rd to the 24th of November, 1654, Blaise Pascal, a philosopher and mathematician of genius, had an experience of God, a kind of mystical ecstasy, which made him into a believer. He was thirty-one years old at the time, about as old as Edward Albee when he wrote his revealing play, *Who's Afraid of Virginia Woolf?* and as old as Albert Schweitzer when, after being a theologian, he became a doctor and founded a leper colony in central Africa. He was as old too as Jesus when he was called and as Isaiah the prophet when he had his vision of God and heard heavenly beings studded with eyes crying out "holy, holy, holy." Clearly something definitive can take place in your life when you are about thirty.

Pascal inscribed his experience of God on parchment and sowed it into his clothes, as if to remind himself physically of this grace every day of his life. This testimony was found on his body when he died nine years later. It reads: "The year of the Lord 1654. Monday, 23 November, from about half past ten in the evening until about half past twelve at night: fire. God of Abraham, God of Isaac, God of Jacob, not the God of philosophers and scholars. Certainty, joy, peace. God of Jesus Christ. He is only found along the ways that are taught in the gospel. Tears of joy. I had parted from him. I fled from him, denied him, crucified him. Let me never be separated from him. Surrender to Jesus Christ."

Most of Pascal's famous thoughts have been superseded by time and by other thinkers, but not this almost chaotic document, this litany of nervous cries, hastily and fervently noted down. This testimony reveals a man whose universe had been shaken and turned upside down and who had been born again, had learnt to speak again.

"God of Abraham, God of Isaac, God of Jacob, not the God of philosophers and scholars."

2.

God is a word in our world, handed down by history. An empty word that everyone can fill up with fantasies and ideas, for example, about the meaning and destiny of his own chance existence. God is a word surrounded by clouds of associations

—youthful memories, church services, a costume, an atmosphere on Sunday, a voice in the upper air;

old man throne invention
absolute invisible power
mistaken idea from primitive times
question-mark stopgap strict father.

Countless people have recognized and expressed their own existential anxiety or their philosophical claims in this word. Everyone who has ever tried to speak about God has always looked above all for formulas for his own soul and its secrets. God has become a name for all that is nameless and unknown in man or for the untraceable origin of the universe or for the vague future which we call death. The most grotesque expectations can be heard in that word—it can mean everything and anything and hardly anybody has ever spoken purely about God. And yet "God" is the only name that I can give to the one whom Israel called the inexpressible and the eternal one, the one who has always found recognition and faith and who still, even now, may perhaps be worthy of faith and who means something to me, with authority and to my joy.

In the book of Israel, the name of God is a story, a series of stories, told again and again, more and more deeply understood, re-interpreted in changing situations and laden with the power of faith and existential experience of countless generations. No one has ever seen God. There are only people who, in the light of an experience that cannot be proved, go on speaking about him. Falteringly, like Moses, who was sent to proclaim the name to his people. He was a stammerer, a man with a speech defect. There are only people who bear witness to him. He is not here. There is only an impossible piece like Psalm 73* and perhaps he is made public in the strength with which words like this are spoken and lived.

With you, I am
always with you.
You hold me tight,
your hand in mine.
You will bring all things
to a good end,
you lead me on
in your good pleasure.
What is heaven
to me without you,
where am I on earth
if you are not there?
Though my body
is broken down,
though my heart dies,
you are my Rock,
my God, the future
that waits for me.
Far away from you
life is not life.

Jesus of Nazareth lives within the sphere of a testimony such as this when he says: "Father, into your hands I commit my spirit."

* All psalms and passages from the psalms quoted in this book are taken from *Fifty Psalms. An Attempt at a New Translation,* by Huub Oosterhuis and others, New York, 1968.

Believing in God, the God of Jesus, is living and continuing to live within the sphere of these words.

3.

There was a time when God was unchangeable. That was when there was still a teaching about faith that consisted of questions and answers and the soul was still regarded as the most important part of man, when half the world's population and certainly a great number of top people in Europe knew, without question, that God was an infinitely perfect spirit.

Unchangeable and unmovable God, who sets everything that is moved in motion, but is, of course, not moved himself —otherwise, where would we be? He showed up well, that God, again and again, to the advantage of certain intellectual and social systems. He was, for instance, an excellent guarantee of unchangeable social relationships for centuries. And he is still, in South Africa and similar places, a white God. In that film of Ingmar Bergman's, *As in a Glass Darkly*, he appears to a psychotic girl in the form of a spider with a stone face, an unmovable mask, a shattering God.

The Bible is supremely contemptuous of unchangeable and unmovable gods. The gods of the pagans, eternal and inexorable truths which crush a man to death, all those subtle reasonings (complete with cast-iron conclusions that nobody can escape from), all those patterns of thought and slogans which dominate man's existence—they are all, according to Israel's experience and idea of faith, masked spiders, gods of silver and gold. They have, Psalm 115 tells us,

mouths, but they cannot speak,
eyes, but they cannot see;

they have ears, but they cannot hear,
and noses, but they cannot smell;
and their hands—they do not feel,
and their feet—they do not walk,
and from their throats, and from their throats
no sound will ever come.
And the man who relies on gods of that kind
is quite as worthless as they are.

The God whom Israel evokes in her psalms, stories and
testimony is far above all these idols. He is known as "reliable
mercy and love, God here among us." He does have feet that
walk and a mouth that speaks and he plays his part in a
movable, rapidly changing world of people whose lives are
short. Psalm 115 bears witness to this—that he is not an
unmovable and unmoved God, but one whose emotions are
affected and who is "blessed" by people: "living men—we
make him happy."

Abraham, Isaac and Jacob, the ancestors of Israel, are described in the Bible as nomads, wandering Aramaeans, roam-
ing around with their clan and their flock in that fertile
territory which curves like a crescent round the Arabian
desert. *Habiru* is what the ancient inscriptions call this kind
of people, outsiders, uprooted people, marginal groups—He-
brews. People who are "present" in the abundant land of
Canaan, socially quite different from the settled population
there. A kind of gypsy people.

It is in this environment of moveable people that we encounter the first traces of the people of the Exodus. The
history of Israel goes back to them.

They were just a handful of people,
a little group of strangers,
homeless, in the midst of pagans,
wanderers, now here, now there,

Psalm 105 tells us. It is from this little group that the God
of Israel "descended"—a God of nomads.

This people of Israel was naturally disposed to believe in
a God who made himself clearly understood, not in the cycle
of the seasons, the fixed and certain and predictable rhythm
of nature, but in the course of history, the dynamic movement
of constantly changing world events.

In Israel's experience, God was always changeable, not to
be fixed in categories, not a number or a definition at our
disposal. He was never a monument of man's imagination, a
splendid, subtle or poetic image of God. You shall not make
any images of me, he tells us. He has a name, but it is unnamable and obscure: I shall be there for you. It could not be
more vague (where then? how?). Unspeakable name, which
means that no man can manipulate it, that it is not at our
disposal like the sound and the letters of a word. That is
why Israel's psalms, prophets and stories always speak of him
in names and visions that are constantly changing. He is un-
predictable and unaccountable—at one moment he is angry
and a moment later he is sorry for it. He is at the same time
both near and yet far. He does not tie himself down and he
does not react mechanically.

In that story of the promise made to Abraham and Sarai
and of the destruction of Sodom and the ten just men, he
is three hungry and tired men and at the same time one

voice, one grim unrelenting God who allows himself to relent,
who never has any change for a pleading, bargaining man,
who lets himself be talked round to mercy. Later on in history,
he is an obscure stranger who wrestles with Jacob in the
night (but Jacob did not learn God's name and always limped
afterwards because of his injured hip). Later still, he is a
burning voice calling to Moses, a gentle breeze comforting
and refreshing Elijah.

God of Abraham, God of Isaac, God of Jacob, not the God
of philosophers and scholars.

He is a pillar of cloud and of fire. He is himself a nomad,
with no stone on which to lay his head and no home, not in
any system. If he lives anywhere, then he does not live in a
temple, but in a tent, just as his people live in tabernacles and
are always going out on journeys and are never sure of their
future. He always goes ahead of his people, who cannot keep
up with him. People always see his back, from behind, like
Moses when he stood in the cleft of the rock and God passed
by him. That is the image par excellence of man's encounter
with God, his experience of God in Israel. Only gradually,
carried along in the movement of our lives, in the course of
our own capricious and usually paradoxical history, do we
ever succeed in tracking him down.

We learn that he is different, that he breaks through our
own obstinate calculations, that he does not fulfill our plans
and is not the philosopher's stone or the cornerstone of our
arguments in suffering. Like Job, perhaps, when he discovered, in opposition to his friends who tried to justify their
ideas of God and their theological views (and thus themselves), that God is different and does not fit in with our

schemes of virtue and reward, guilt and retribution, that he does not fill up our gaps and is no comfort when we cannot go on and reach the limits of our existence. He is not God as we think of him.

People who know that they themselves are greater than any scheme, who do not allow themselves to be fixed down to anything and allow their future and their growth to be denied, people who hope that they will not be nailed down to their past, which is often wicked, and that they will not be caught up in the machinery of vengeance and disgrace—it sometimes occurs to such people that this God is recognizable and credible, and it seems right to sing that he is grace and forgiveness, a God of people.

Those who want to know about him prefer to live precariously and restlessly rather than frozen, homeless rather than riveted to what is past. In that experience of life, perhaps they receive and recognize, in the long run, the inexpressible name of God.

4.

The Bible has preserved testimonies to God from all the phases of Israel's history, from the time that the nation was still in its infancy until its exile and decline centuries later. A child believes in muscles, in fighting and winning. When Israel was a child, it felt and reacted as a child. During Israel's childhood, God was a fighting God, stronger than all the other gods. In the oldest part of the Bible he is called a "hero in war" who sets upon his enemies "screaming like a woman in childbirth." An immature and primitive world is

expressed in a primitive testimony of faith. In the beginning
he is in Israel as militant, as revengeful and as ghostly as all
the gods of men, carrying the ten plagues of Egypt in his
knapsack, a demanding God who exacts punishment and
revenge. But, together with Israel, he makes history and he
grows and changes and becomes more human. The God who
reveals himself in the liberation of the house of slavery, who
creates greater scope and freedom for his people, becomes, in
his association with Israel, more and more "different from all
other gods." He becomes less and less an "idol"—demanding,
violent, powerful, a scheme or system forcing and oppressing
people—and more and more a person who can leave other
people free, a father who can let his children go.

He becomes more and more liberation.

When Israel becomes a man, it puts aside its childish
dreams. Its adult testimony is to a God who thinks thoughts of
peace, not of destruction, just as a grown man who has learnt
from life no longer believes in violence, in fighting and winning, in striking and punishing, but in patience and forgiveness.

This mature testimony is to a God who no longer forces,
who is more and more modest and powerless. He accompanies
his people into exile—his people, his son on earth, is banished
abroad, belittled, destroyed. He is impotent and all the idols
and powers, all the gods who insist that things must be like
this and in no other way, are more powerful than he is. There
is no more temple and no more prophets and he is silent.
Only a wretched little group, a remnant in Israel, still recognizes him. Among them, the expectation is born that this
God will ultimately make himself known and speak in the
form of a servant, someone who does not demand anything

from you, who bears and suffers. That God, who humiliates and empties himself infinitely to give freedom to people, who does not want to fight men but serve them—that God appeared and spoke, scripture has testified, in Jesus of Nazareth. The God who became less and less in the course of Israel's history and more and more a God along whose way you can go, who is not absolute and not a blinding truth, but relative and escapable—that God makes his will and his intentions, his ideas of peace and his name fully known by becoming the God of Jesus.

Jesus, a son of men, is one of many men, without form or splendor. He lives a long way away and fails, falling into the hands of men. We no longer feel the scandal that this crucified man was to his followers and to strangers. He dies—because of a foolish misunderstanding. If the God of Israel has spoken "for ever" in him and he is called God's word to this world, what is that God making known to us? That he does not demand anything from us. That he wants to liberate us and serve us, makes no demands, does not want any sacrifices, does not want to see any blood. That he prefers men to lose him and forget him rather than be bowed down underneath him. That he wants to disappear and be dead, so that we may live.

Those who, in Israel or anywhere else, bear witness to this God and are called to interpret his words and pass them on speak the only language which is really daringly equal to him, which does justice to him and gives him free scope—the language of myth and poetry. The language of concealment —saying what cannot be said and yet has to be said, again and again and always in a different way. A language in which the mystery of that God is not seized hold of, mastered and subdued, in which God does not become my property. A language in which I do not force him to yield and he does not force me to believe. God, who leaves me free, speaks to me in a language of freedom and respect, does not overwhelm me with strong terms, but gives me his name like a song and a story, in images and likenesses. A language which has power and which works outside all logic and far transcends all logic. A language in which a man can grow and in which he has time, all his life.

5.

All words are relative and anyone who tries to manage without words is not a man. We can rely on ourselves, saying one thing at one time and something else at another.

What can divide us now
from God who is so near?
In death there is no threat,
the future holds no fear.

At one moment we can sing this, almost triumphantly and quite at our ease (because we are all singing together) and a moment later come up against Psalm 22, for example: God, my God, why have you abandoned me?

All words are no more than words and they all have their special time, when they are powerful and indispensable, but they do not remain permanently in force, every day of our lives and every century of history.

There have been centuries when men boldly took on God,

radiantly and simply, and dared to adorn his name, in all
sincerity and in glowing faith, with mighty epithets like
omniscient and omnipresent. Centuries when people were
able to fill great words such as this with their faith and to
express themselves and recognize themselves in them.

No one is called upon to judge the centuries or to set them
off one against the other. All we have to do is to live in our
own century—and our century does not get on easily with
such radiant epithets for God. Perhaps all words applied to
him are too great for us.

God is not someone great and glorious
with power and majesty
he has no position, no first place
nowhere in this world.
No one becomes better because of God
he is no use to anyone, misery is still misery
he does not mend you when you are broken
he does not intervene in any dispute
(not even in the church)
he is not "the answer to every question"
(as a popular religious teenage song
would like him to be)
he does not solve anything
there in Southeast Asia
between Washington and Hanoi

You must love him
as he is:
not a God, not a spirit,
not a person, not an image,
Eckhart said
in the thirteenth century.

He is not the light of day
but darkness and emptiness
he is not a high tree of life
but a shapeless branch
he is not the immense sea
but a cup of water at the most
a spoonful of water to combat thirst.
He is not a mighty voice
but a vulnerable silence.
Lonely and despairing God,
like a man who is looking for another man
and cannot find him:

"Really I believe nothing
and doubt everything, even you.
But sometimes, whenever I think
    that you really live,
then I think that you are love and lonely
and that, in the same despair, you are looking for me
as I am for you."
This experience of God,
expressed here by G. K. van het Reve,
is also a fact in history.
The poor and the exiled, humiliated people,
mystics and near heretics, inside and outside the churches,
have, in the course of the centuries, sometimes
looked for words like this:

impossible God, God with a name of nothing,
little God who cannot hold his own
against people,
against their gods of money and violence.
God of Jesus.

What will always happen to him
is what happened
to the powerless man from Nazareth.
He goes the way of every seed,
he is always the least of men.
All poverty is the poverty of God,
everything that is small and humiliated
reminds us of him.

Believing, praying is
enduring with the God of Jesus
or, according to Bonhoeffer,
sharing in the suffering of God
participating in the impotence of God
in this world.

God is dead. A vague fashionable term?

Words that take you unawares. Even for those who use
them, there is something mysterious and troubled about them.
They surprise you while you are speaking them. What you say
frightens you—what do I really mean? But, at this moment,
there are perhaps no other words which really do justice to
what you are experiencing.

Perhaps the words "God is dead" mean that we live with
him as we live with our dead—in deprivation and in ques-
tioning, near and yet far, in waiting and in silence, in
memories. A dead person is forced to rely on our memory of
him. He is not here, moves farther and farther back into the
past, is lost in forgetfulness and sorrow. Only the reverence
of memory can still reach him.

"But I Am Always Smaller Than My Song"

1.

Be glad and remember the Lord here among us
and let us be thankful for all he has done—
his life here on earth, his death and resurrection.
The first of many brothers is God's own Son.

He emptied himself of all honor and glory,
fulfilling the will of his Father to save,
and being a man, he gave himself by dying.
The first-born of creation became our slave.

The meaning of life here is living for others,
but how could we do this if he had not shown
that he was the way of love and total service
and by our love of others we should be known.

You, first among men, were defenceless and lonely,
becoming like seed lying dead in the ground.

Now you are our bread—let us be bread for all men
by giving to our fellows the life we've found.

2.

The man who wants to live the life of a god on earth
must go the way
of every seed
and die before he has rebirth.

For he must understand what going this way implies—
to share the life
and destiny
of everything that lives and dies.

And like the smallest seed exposed to the sun and rain
he has to die
in wind and storm
before he comes to life again.

The grain of wheat can yield no harvest until it's dead—
it too must die
for other men
to be each others' living bread.

And this is what our God himself has already done—
he lived and died
as man on earth
to give new life to everyone.

3.

God does not send us his word
like a great torrent of water

raging in tempest and flood
sweeping us blindly along,

but like a glimpse of the sun
or a green branch in the winter,
rain falling softly on earth:
this is how God comes to us.

Stripped of all beauty and form
God comes to us as a servant,
suffering here in this world,
dying that we may find life.

Stranger unknown in our midst,
he is a name without power.
Those who are open to peace
welcome his name in their hearts.

He restores sight to the blind,
those who are deaf now can hear him.
This is the news that he brings:
happy the man who believes.

God does not hide from our sight,
we need not look up to heaven.
He is with us here on earth,
living as man among men.

Gently he asks for our faith,
seeking consent to his message;
here in our life and our death,
we become people of God.

4.

You are a son of men and one of us,
blood of our blood, of our own generation.

You are our God, but no stranger to us;
you share our happiness and all our sorrow.
When we were nowhere, but living in death,
you alone kindled a light in our darkness.

We are your people and light of your light,
people of light, but our ways are still hidden.

People of flesh and stone, hoping, afraid;
God, take us home, give us peace, we beseech you.

5.

At last night is ending,
the day is drawing near.

The people living in the night
will see the long-awaited light.
Rising in darkness from afar,
it shines on them, the morning star.

The son of man will come once more,
not as a child, obscure and poor;
only the Father knows the day,
all we must do is watch and pray.

Though sun and moon may cease to shine,
we who believe will know his sign:

this is when we will understand
his second coming is at hand.

In winter when the tree seems dead,
we have to hope and look ahead
to the green branch that will appear
when summer and new life are near.

Exposed to every wind and storm,
deprived of beauty and of form,
but we who live in faith know well
that branch is called Emmanuel.

God with us is a living name,
he will not put our faith to shame,
if we are open to receive
the Son in whom we all believe.

At last night is ending,
the day is drawing near.

6.

As long as there are men and women,
as long as earth has fruit to give,
so long will you be God our Father—
we thank you for all things that live.

As long as human words are spoken
and man lives for his fellow man,
so long will you be here among us
who share the work your love began.

You feed the birds, you clothe the flowers,
you know your creatures and their ways.
O Lord, you are our home, our refuge
and you have numbered all our days.

You are our light, our life unending;
we seem to die, but are not dead.
You sent your only Son to save us—
his body is our living bread.

So all that you, God, have created
must worship you while life endures.
You are the love that gave us being,
accept us, Lord, for we are yours.

7.

What is this place where we are meeting?
Only a house, the earth its floor,
walls and a roof sheltering people,
windows for light, an open door.
Yet it becomes a body that lives
when we are gathered here
and know our God is near.

Words from afar, stars that are falling,
sparks that are sown in us like seed,
names for our God, dreams, signs and wonders
sent from the past are all we need.
We in this place remember and speak
again what we have heard:
God's free redeeming word.

And we accept bread at his table,
broken and shared, a living sign.
Here in this world, dying and living,
we are each others' bread and wine.
This is the place where we can receive
what we need to increase
God's justice and his peace.

Letters About Faith to a Cradle Catholic

I believe.
I—triumphantly conscious of myself?
I—lonely? I—at my own risk?
or modestly: I for myself?
Who am I?
A name, a history, wearing a suit,
a position, an identity card.
An invisible interior,
drawbacks.
Hidden ambitions, conflicting voices and dreams,
A little bit of life in the plural.
Changeable I, chance I.
"I is another":
the cry of the French poet Rimbaud
in the middle of the nineteenth century,
long before Freud and Fellini,
comes from every man.
I believe.

Believing is not saying yes, with your head bowed and your
eyes shut, to everything that is shot at you by a centuries-old

ecclesiastical authority. For example, that the Church of Rome is the only possible church, that the medieval formulation of the Eucharist is the only true one or that the experience of marriage as prescribed by the pope is the only permissible one.

To regard all kinds of doctrines and rules as absolutely certain, not only in the world of religion, but also in the ethical and social sphere—people can do it and do do it; indeed, for a very great number of people, it is the only safe course in a complicated world.

And who would wish to deny them their right to this safety? But "believing" is really more than this.

The believer is a man who can stand up and, with open eyes and not as a subordinate, entrust himself to another man. Taking others on trust, letting yourself be touched and called, appealed to by others, allowing yourself to be taught by and being amenable to what comes to you, having the courage to expect something from another person—that attitude is known as faith.

Believing is intimately related to growing and maturity. Just as a mature man can, throughout the whole of his life, grow in people, in togetherness with them, and can have a history with other people. Just as he can become more and more deeply involved in that event that we call "human existence," something that is much greater than anything that I for myself or I at my own risk can ever grasp.

Whoever you may be and however old or however young you may be, your real place is in that relationship and you know this, spontaneously and intuitively. You are not that critical doubter who is on his guard all the time against deceit and trickery, who distrusts everything that is said and who holds himself aloof from everything that happens, watching carefully, but preferably out of range. Nor are you that self-satisfied little person who is the source of all knowledge and who does not have to be told anything. You have to depend on everything and everybody. You have to be carried along and pushed by the words and the strength of others. Above all, you have to rely on that mature ingenuousness with which others believe in you and expect something from you.

Not believing is no longer seeing anything in sharing and communication with other people, not expecting anything more from them, no longer listening to them. Not believing is thinking that nothing means anything to you any more. Sometimes we cause other people not to believe—someone who is never spoken to, never expects anything from others, is never sad, ceases to believe. Where there is no longer any inspiration and creativity between people there is no faith.

Faith is creative. Your faith in another person evokes the truth that is in him. Anyone who has friends, and, I should imagine, anyone who has children will know this from experience—that believing is a way to life. This faith will save us, far more than all the technical and artistic miracles that we perform. Is this real? Is it anything more than a plea for what is commonly known as "credulity," a rather naïve, "love-in" kind of optimism? Ought we not to behave a little more carefully in this hard world?

"Believing" is taking a risk and only experience will prove whether it is human and humane. You have to try it out, live it experimentally.

If I am asked to commit my whole soul, I shall quite rightly be very demanding. If what is at stake is a commitment for the whole of my life, to somebody or to several people, I shall need a great deal of faith. I shall sometimes want to experience quite deeply that I am not entrusting myself in vain. At least now and then I shall want to know empirically whether other people are responding to my trust, my expectation, whether they are really "worthy of faith."

If nothing can ever be heard, I cannot go on listening. If you never experience life lived as something genuinely human, then you cannot go on believing in the long run that it can be lived.

I can well imagine somebody saying: I myself believe that it is possible to be a human being, again and again. I believe it on the basis of all that I see and hear and all that I have heard from many other people and from many previous centuries. I am very vulnerable in that faith—I know doubt and despair and many painful experiences contradict me and make me falter. But I hope it will succeed, that it will be given to me.

A time for searching, a time for losing;
a time for mourning, a time for dancing;
a time for silence, a time for speaking,
a time for loving, a time for hating,*

said the Jewish preacher who put down his sometimes rather tired and bitter verses on paper about two hundred years before Christ.

A time for yes and a time for no; a time for this way and

* This and all other passages and readings from the Bible are based on the author's own versions, with reference to the original texts and to existing modern translations.

a time for that, quite a different way. And all these times,
hours and moments together make up one human life.

Even for those who believe in God there is a time for yes
and a time for no.

A time for living with him, a time for forgetting him. A
time for knowing who he is (and that he is, now, for me) and
a time for despair, alienation.

Everything has its time. This means, for example, that
life cannot be forced. Happiness and unhappiness, joy and
death—you just have it. It is not at your disposal. No human
being is at your disposal. No one's heart can be compelled
to love. That is the experience of life. God is not at your
disposal. That is the experience of faith.

God is not always true. He cannot always be lived, believed.
You cannot always worship him, bless him.

My God, you fathom my heart and you know me—
you have laid your hand upon me—
I am your creation in my bones and tissues—

These words of Psalm 139 do not always hold good. Sometimes, when you are carried away, you recognize them and
you care for them. At other times, they are a threat. Most of
the time, they mean nothing to you.

At some time in your life, there may be a moment of being
known, of being secure in God. Then the words of a psalm
like this may preserve the memory of this experience (or of
this illusion?). Faith is not a constant in your emotions or in
the thoughts at the back of your mind. It is not a possession.
It is a to-and-fro between yes and no.

Anyone who really lives with other people, with friends

and loved ones, and who lives with God will recognize the
words of the poetess Vasalis:

I feel the freedom of a great love
which makes room for doubt, despair and absence.

"In those days" (the story is in the second chapter of
Mark's gospel): four men lift the roof off a house in a
Jewish village for their paralyzed friend and then lower him,
together with his bed, through a trapdoor or something in
front of the feet of Jesus of Nazareth who is there preaching
the word.

Then it says, "seeing their faith." Faith can be discerned
in all kinds of resourceful or clumsy things that men do.

"Seeing their faith"—the faith of all these men—Jesus said
to the paralytic, "Your sins are forgiven."

Apparently the faith of your friends is as beneficial to you
and as liberating as your own faith.

Your own faith or not being able to believe may not even
be so very important. You can be saved by the faith of others.

"Others carry my burden and the power of others becomes
my strength. The faith of the Church helps my fear," said
Luther, in whom faith was born again in a new form and
in new words four centuries ago.

It is possible—letting yourself be carried by the faith of
others, who take you where you do not perhaps even want
to go, yielding to others, who drag you along with them to
God. This happened when you were very young and had no
will of your own—your parents had you baptized and brought
up with the name of God and Jesus. And now you are a
Christian and simply cannot get out of it. Just as you learned,

from your earliest childhood, how to love other people and
you cannot stop doing it now. It is possible—attaching yourself
to a community that prays, while you yourself . . . Leading
a community in prayer, while you yourself . . . Not knowing,
but still joining in. Not being able to believe, but still . . .
Being dead, perhaps, but still living.

People believe with and for each other, always. In each
other's name. In that remarkable and difficult community of
Christians at Corinth, twenty or thirty years after Jesus'
death, people seem to have been in the habit of having themselves baptized for a dead person (a counterpart, so to speak,
to infant baptism, which has been, since time immemorial, an
unfailing intuition of faith in the Church). We too believe,
learn how to believe, in our dead. We are at one with them
in the faith with which they clung to God. And because
their voices are silent, we believe and call in their name that
God is not a God of the dead, but of living people.

"I don't think a man is a simpleton because he believes in
God," Lucebert once said to Bibeb, referring to Simon Vin-
kenoog.

What being a believer is and how it works becomes clear in
the way people call, pray and live with each other. There
are different ways of believing, just as there are very many
different generations and types of people. There are people
who believe very positively: I believe in . . . , in . . . , all
the twelve articles of the creed, a hundred and one feelings
and ideas, venerable because they have been lived for centuries. There are also, it would seem, people who believe with
a lot of pain and bother, who are always recalcitrant and never

wholehearted in their faith. Faith is where one man respects the other man and leaves him in freedom to follow his own way. Faith is keeping the group together, learning to live with one's exact opposite, the person who votes against you, and knowing that life is more powerful than any doctrine.

Believing is making do with what is there, taking the facts seriously, believing your eyes. But it is also being rebellious, "disbelieving," not putting up with the situation as you find it. Saying "and yet." Not being able to believe that World Press photo of 1966—a dead Vietnamese tied behind an American tank, Hector being dragged behind the chariot of his victorious enemy, that World Press photo of 1967—now years older, years of hunger, that World Press photo of 1969? 1970? 1980? Not being able to believe that any one of us is born to tie another man to his tank, to die like that.

"Believing in God" is being drawn by him. It is "grace." That is a vertical word. It is not popular. It is usually handled too quickly and too easily. Faith is grace.

A person can experience faith in himself almost as a wonder that happens by chance. He has not bred it himself and he cannot cherish it and preserve it. It is suggested to him. He says, I believe in God. I cannot help it and I do not know how it came about. No one can believe, Jesus says, unless the Father draws him to faith.

A Song, a Didactic Poem About Life

Based on Ecclesiastes

1.

Everything that is under heaven
has its time and all things have their hour.
There is a time for living and dying,
a time for killing, a time for healing.

A time for planting, a time for uprooting,
a time for breaking, a time for building,
a time for crying, a time for laughing,
a time for mourning, a time for dancing.

A time for throwing stones away,
a time for gathering them up,
a time for embracing, a time for continence,
a time for searching, a time for losing.

A time for preserving, a time for disposing,
a time for silence, a time for speaking,
a time for loving, a time for hating,
a time for war, a time for peace.

He has placed his name upon the world
and eternity in the heart of man,
but who can fathom what happens there,
for everything is deep and beyond our reach.

What exists today—it has long been there,
and what will be existed before
and what has happened happens again
and God looks again for what has gone past.

2.

A generation goes and another comes,
only the earth remains.
The sun rises and the sun sets,
then out of breath it begins again.

Restlessly changing the wind chases
first to the south, then to the north.
All the rivers flow to the sea,
and yet the sea is never full.

All these things are inexpressible,
all these restlessly striving things;
men's eyes never have their fill of seeing,
men's ears never have their fill of hearing.

In the past and now—who can explain it?
who knows if love awaits him or hatred?
the living know that we shall die,
the dead know nothing at all.

Let man then always be happy
as long as he lives under the sun,

eating and drinking and making friends,
doing what he can find for his hands to do,

before one shower follows another,
before the notes of the song are silenced,
before the doors are shut for ever
and the pitcher is broken at the spring.

Nineveh   Corinth   Amsterdam

It is not for us
to define the day,
but he will come
and men will once again be called
to proclaim the word of God
in such a way
that it will change and renew the world.
                              Bonhoeffer

In the midst of all the inexplicable events which we call
the world, the world of today, it remains an impenetrable fact
that the gospel is still proclaimed and still finds a response.
Although it has been questioned and challenged, it has apparently been lived for twenty centuries and it has spread.
And it is apparently still at work in the activities and thoughts
of countless people. People, just people, know or feel that
they are called and drawn by the testimony about Jesus of
Nazareth. There are twelve of them, perhaps, or seventy or
three thousand, and throughout the whole of the world and
all the centuries they are a vast number that no one can

count. They are a handful of people in one of the hundred and fifty churches where you live.

A church is a point of contact for people who believe, in other words, who see a future and salvation in that man with his God and cling to him.

They go to a church, week by week perhaps, to hear a word that will throw light on their lives. The gospel is unfolded and laid open. There is a sermon.

Everything to do with the Churches today and especially their structure, their hierarchy and almost all their authoritative statements are problematical, disputable and obscure. Not, however, the meeting round the gospel. If what is said there is good and human, the deepest meaning of the Church —possibly even against the Church—takes place there.

Anyone who is the spokesman in a Church—ordained priest, called preacher or ordinary man or woman—has to realize that he has not been "set apart" from people and appointed to proclaim the Church with her laws and practices or to preach the pope or the prestige of Christianity or the right of Chalcedon, but to go on speaking the gospel, in other words, to speak about God.

While I am speaking, I evoke the reality. The form of my words, the key, the aggressiveness or the modesty of my story, the power or the boredom in my voice—these determine the way in which the reality appears, whether it is credible or in vain, whether it is human or not. God will appear in the way in which I speak about him. He is made present in words— and the effect of words can never be calculated or entirely known.

How will God appear when I preach about the biological virginity of Mary or the natural law or the bloodless sacrifice of the Eucharist?

Speaking about God is above all: "Who or what is God?" Evoking that question, in opposition to all self-assured answers, and keeping it alive, obstinately and disturbingly.

Every religion has its holy places, around which the vast space of heaven and earth is arranged. Holy mountain (the earth's navel), holy tree, holy spring, temple, hearth or grave —all these are places where man can orientate himself in a world that is too vast for him to envisage, places where he can meet gods who have at one time revealed themselves there and who will, now or in the future, appear there again.

The point of orientation for those who believe in Jesus of Nazareth is not a holy grave or a holy Mount Calvary, nor is some religious Pentagon, St. Peter's in Rome or some other temple the holy place to which they feel themselves to be drawn and which establishes and puts in order the infinite space of this world, past and future, for them.

For these believers, Jesus' "life story" is the place where God appears. For them, the holy ground is the gospel and the words which this man spoke about God. God is to be encountered (perhaps now or at some time) where that story in Jesus' name is proclaimed and told again, sung and prayed. And God can appear as the creator and father of man's existence and man becomes visible as the image and likeness of God where words are spoken in Jesus' spirit and in accordance with his discipline in order to interpret man's existence.

To put it in black and white, in good Protestant terms, my orientation in this world is not the Holy See, but the proclamation of the gospel.

The only way of proclaiming the gospel is to speak about God and men as Jesus of Nazareth did. Jesus, in what he says, continues the story of Israel, his people's wisdom and piety, their faith and their experience of God. He moves in scripture and gives his consent to the orientation that is written there in songs and stories. He understands and unfolds the mystery of man's being according to the tradition of the law and the prophets.

Israel is man. The mystery of Israel is the mystery of every man and the God of Israel is the Lord of all. We who meet together, in a church, to listen are Israel—Abraham without a son, Jacob with the angel, David who kills Uriah, Job (but nameless and unreconciled), Joseph in the well. We are the psalms, blessing and cursing.

Preaching should arouse the happiness of that recognition, mediate and make connections between then and now, far away and near, tradition and the present time. It should be attuned to and play upon what is there in the circle of those present at the meeting. It should place these people here and now within the sphere of what has been reality since time immemorial—we are that man.

Luke's gospel has preserved a piece of preaching in which the most distinctive voice of Jesus is echoed:

What father among you
would hand his son a stone
when he asked for bread?

Or hand him a snake instead of a fish?
Or hand him a scorpion
if he asked for an egg?
If you then, who are evil,
know how to give your children what is good,
how much more will the heavenly Father
give the Holy Spirit
to those who ask him!

People are here referred back to their own unpretentious everyday lives. They are no better than they are—"you who are evil" is stated quite boldly. But there is no accusation and there is no enlargement of the statement. There is simply a proclamation that people, for all their shortcomings, are still good enough to be the image of God. The dimension of men's ordinary lives is illuminated and people are encouraged and strengthened in what they are. In his edition of the Hassidic writings, Martin Buber showed clearly that this form of preaching was the charisma of Judaism.

Preaching must make people great, do justice to them and respect them. It must proclaim grace. Reveal whatever grace there is in people and call it by its name and not accuse them or belittle them. Preaching must point out humanity, hand men on to their fellow men, make one man recognizable to another man, open people's eyes to what is happening in themselves, bear witness to what men have seen and heard, that there are people in this world who do not hate, but who are committed to the cause of peace. It must say: you are not far from the kingdom of God.

Preaching is the teaching of an attitude, the evocation of the possibilities of faith and the forms in which it appears.

It does not solve very much and does not provide many answers. But it tries to liberate a power in the listener, so that he himself becomes responsible. It does not impose any views or compel consent. It is, among all the words that are spoken in this world, an offer that can be freely accepted or rejected. It speaks the defenseless language of the parables.

But it also speaks the language of prophecy—it intervenes in man himself, between his actions and his conscience, between the person he himself thinks he is and the person God intends him to be. It contradicts people when they persist in their own way of life (which tells them that the problems of world hunger and the armaments race cannot be solved, that things have always been the same, that we do not need to be healed or forgiven).

Preaching breaks through a deadly silence, asks questions when men seek refuge in certainties, defies the bitterness with which they admit defeat in the face of the existing order, the status quo. It calls men back from the established patterns of language they use to speak about God and good and evil, the language in which they wander about like prisoners, but which they firmly maintain and impose on others. Despite all the arguments and phrases and principles, despite all the gods and powers that tyrannize over us, preaching proclaims the name of the God of Jesus, who is greater and more human than all our objections and ideas.

He is for us the God of the powers,
a God of men—

These words from Psalm 46 form the refrain of preaching: that he liberates us, promises to give a new name, new birth, to people who were born long ago, who have for a long time been the captives of their names and their adult bodies.

Matthew's gospel sees the fulfillment of what is said in Psalm 78 in Jesus' preaching:

I will speak to you in parables
and expound things hidden since the foundation of the world.

Jesus proclaims the coming of the kingdom of God in the parable of the little bit of yeast that leavens three measures of flour (almost nine gallons, enough for a meal for a hundred and fifty people) all through until it can be eaten, or in the parable of the smallest of all seeds that grows into a great tree. What mystery, hidden from the very beginning of time and still hidden again and again, does Jesus reveal in these parables? The paradoxical mystery of man—that, however insignificant he may be, he still has a future.

This is what preaching tells us: God himself is coming in the wretched here-and-now of people, simply people. Here and now, in my insignificant and vulnerable situation, his reality is revealed (his "kingdom," in the language of the gospels), just as he appeared in the chance fate of Jesus of Nazareth, folly and a stumbling block, not God as we think of him.

Preaching preserves that vision of hope.

A person is appointed to preach, ordained. He does not simply take it up himself as something that he "will just do." It is given to him as a task by others, by the authorities—he is allowed to preach. And when he begins to act as spokesman in the community, he does so in the conviction that someone

has to do this—everyone cannot call, bear witness and proclaim the gospel at the same time. He is the mouth of the
community. He can be this and is allowed to be, insofar as
he is one of the circle of people and insofar as the faith of
all of them is expressed in him. His appointment is also made
on the basis of his suitability—he must, for example, have a
voice that can be heard, he must want to go on telling that
story about God. He will have to find the self-discipline to
carry on understanding and interpreting scripture.

To do this, he will have to dissociate himself more and
more from the theological language of his training. Just as
he will also have to go on setting himself free from all the
positions in the Church and in society into which he will
constantly find himself maneuvered as a man of God, at the
expense of his freedom of speech, and from all the expectations and demands that will enclose him like a cocoon—a
priest, a minister, has to behave like this, has to be that. A
man who cannot be very obstinate about this should not take
on this "office."

Above all, he must be psychologically equal to the task,
so that he can, when the time comes, be uninteresting or
ridiculous in telling this story. He must be able to put up
with the folly of the proclamation of the gospel.

He will find it in turn a fine task and a meaningless one.
Sometimes he will be afraid to open his mouth, like Paul in
Corinth. Sometimes he will hate it, like Jonah in Nineveh.
As time goes by, he will have very few illusions left about it.
His words will often be understood in quite a different way
from what he intended—they will end up in a pattern of
ideas and a sphere of emotions in which they cause misunder-
standing instead of illumination, discussion instead of con-

solation. Nor will he know what will become of it all, even though he may be encouraged by the wisdom of the peasant, who goes to sleep once he has sown his seed.

His words will have no special value and most of what he says cannot be proved. They are also not the finest words, like the New Testament, which is certainly not the finest of all literature, but a laborious and often rather disorderly story —when you read it, you cannot help suspecting that its authors did not really bring it off entirely.

Once he has been appointed, he has the task of providing services for church-going people who are in the habit of ful-filling their Sunday duty and preach to them if they ever get as far as wanting to hear a good word. As every preacher realizes, that phrase "church-going" implies a number of problems. He will have to deal with every conceivable out-of-date and wrong feeling and idea which has, in the past, been instilled into the immature consciences of people who have not achieved independence and which now haunts the minds of those people like a resentment or a neurosis, despite the fact that they would otherwise like to believe in the gospel.

Sometimes he will have to free people from every recollec-tion of the word "God" so that they will depart greatly re-lieved and "no longer believing." In that case, it may mean that he is there simply to proclaim redemption to captives.

Sometimes, however, he will have a different experience. As he pronounces the name of God and reads and comments on the gospel in a community of people who somehow believe (however faulty and inhibited that faith may be), a reality may be expressed which is greater and more profound than any that he, as the leader of the community who happens to be there, can ever evoke. He himself, the one who is speaking, and the people, those who hear this word, may be drawn into a relationship and a dialogue, into a covenant of speaking and hearing, which is unlimited and gratuitous and trustworthy and which has meaning in itself. Sometimes he will know, to his great joy, that he is allowed to be the mediator of this experience of God.

Guilt and Forgiveness

Grown men have a knowledge of evil and an understanding and the necessary experience of the seamy side of each others' lives. They are aware of the chain reaction of misunderstanding and the infallible mechanism of "from bad to worse." On a small scale there is the broken marriage, with its usual consequence of unhappy children. On a large scale there is the destructive peace treaty of 1918 which drove an entire nation into embittered isolation, sowing the seeds of new violence which bore fruit twenty years later, and even today that nation is obsessed by an immense feeling of guilt, a great hole in the lives of millions of people.

As in the narrow sphere of our own lives, so too in the wider sphere of the history of an entire people, of mankind as a whole—we can never put our finger on the exact moment when guilt is born. It is only when we look back that we see guilt, that we see human failings which can be accounted for and episodes which are in themselves perhaps innocent, but which seem to have led to unaccountable crimes.

When does guilt have its beginning? Where and when does it begin in man, so that he allows himself to be swept along by a destructive system like that of the Nazis?

There is no answer to this question. The origin of guilt is lost in obscurity. The process of its growth too is just as complicated—the personal frustrations of so many, perhaps quite decent and well-meaning people, who influence each other and become involved with each other under the pressure of so many different social factors and then become a power, a fate for more and more people, still more and more people and so on and so on. One of those people may perhaps have been called Gertrud Slotke, the sad figure at the center of the Munich trials of 1966, a single woman of sixty-four, who simply could not plead guilty. What was the extent of the wrongs done to her by others that made it impossible for her to escape from that isolation of silence, not knowing, flight and getting rid of her guilt on to others?

Sometimes a person recognizes himself in the guilt and crime of others and experiences his own inborn impotence or unconsciously cherished shortcomings as the possible beginning of moral disruption. We recognize this and that it may happen in this way. What is present in me, what can I do in the lives of other people? Sometimes we can foresee the guilt that we are able to take on ourselves and this becomes a source of anxiety. We all know what it is to be ashamed of what is present in people.

The inescapable interconnection of all people in evil, that bitter experience, is portrayed in the biblical myth of the fall. That story, too well known to Christianity and all too frequently misunderstood, does not try to provide an explanation for the mysterious origin of evil, nor does it aim to tell how it all happened then, a long time ago. What we see above all in the story of Adam, who was, in the language of the Bible, the man of all times, everyman, is what is happening now, inexplicably but really. Man, fashioned of dust from the soil, that man is made free. He gives names to his world. He is given another person and there is love and recognition. Then, in this living together, evil happens. Evil does not come into the world from God, as in the ancient oriental myths or the Greek tragedies. God is not the guilty one—man is guilty. Evil happens from man to man—people draw each other along and they are together responsible. "Original sin" is the name that we give to this solidarity in evil. We say "original sin," not so that we can explain evil in ourselves as a matter of biological heredity, but in order to indicate that each one of us has his special place in that event, that each one of us has "unclean hands."

"There are no just people," Albert Camus once said. "There are only people who are to some extent poor in justice. The worst criminal and the most upright judge stand shoulder to shoulder. Both are equally wretched and in this they are at one with one another." One of the witnesses at the Auschwitz trial gave a very concrete meaning to the difficult concept of "original sin" when he said, "I should only like to remind you of how many people stood watching at their doors when we were driven out of our houses and loaded on to the cattle trucks." As the gospel tells us, "If there is one of you who has not sinned, let him be the first to throw a stone." And Paul, in his own grim and radical way of speaking, says in his letter to the Romans, "Every mouth may be stopped and the whole world may be held guilty."

The whole world. That has a pitiless sound and the conclusion is inescapable—we are all of us left out in the cold, in the desert. In the history of Christianity, this idea has defeated many people and it certainly contains more than

enough to make people feel assailed, predetermined and paralyzed in every aspect of their existence. What, then, ought
to be the attitude of people who have been born without
suspecting anything at all and who simply carry on with their
lives, with other people, in this world which is held guilty?
I suspect that the answer to this question has already been
given to us in a living example, possibly in as many people
as there have been cases in which the guilt of the world and
the power of evil have been encountered by us. The answer,
then, is that there are people who simply begin, somewhere
in the "whole world," to be responsible for one other person,
a few other people, a family or a wide circle of people in
their environment. There are people who make a beginning
where their entire environment is paralyzed, who break
through a deadly silence, who stand up where others sit down
in impotence, people to whom you can appeal and who reply,
understand and radiate strength, people who still manage
to do good, even with their unclean hands. There are people
who go and stand out in the cold, in the desert, in that guilt,
who believe that they do not have the right to dissociate
themselves from it and get rid of it on to others. Sometimes
you meet such people, in Germany, in church, in some part
of the world. They probably do not say, "This is all my fault,
my guilt"—the situation is too complicated for that. What they
say is, "I am involved in this," and take the situation as their
point of departure and see that this is where their responsibility begins.

The moment when a man has this insight and makes this
choice is a moment of being called. It is as though he becomes
aware of a voice calling him to being, responsibly, a man and

as though he at the same time experiences within himself the strength to answer this call.

And, the moment he makes this choice, he really encounters the power of evil. Then, for the first time, he experiences fully how heavily laden the world is, how completely at a deadlock the situation is. From now on, he is fighting a losing battle. He is really in the desert, among wild animals, fears and temptations of fatalism and doubt. He is tossed to and fro between conflicting thoughts—what is the use and where shall I make a start, what will become of it and it is simply an illusion. The more deeply a person becomes involved in that world and the more intensely concerned he becomes in the fate of others, the more violently he is challenged and tested. The man who does not accept responsibility is not put to the test. The man who does not believe is not affected by doubts about faith. The man who believes in God, in people, is thrown into doubt and uncertainty. The man who carries another man with all his wretchedness around his neck is tempted—it is pointless, I will get rid of him, I will drop him. But there are people who do not get rid of others like this and do not dissociate themselves from them. They say, "Your guilt, your seamy side is there, that evil in you, but it does not matter to me that you are like that—I accept you, I forgive you." There are such people and they are often here among us in the concrete—parents with children, a man and wife living with each other in good and in bad times. There are Jews who have survived the concentration camp and who have lost everyone and everything and who, without behaving naïvely or wanting to justify anything, still do not hate. People who have been purified so much that they are totally unselfish in their trust in this world, and give this trust for nothing.

Wherever this strength—we call it forgiveness—is visible, the fatality of evil is broken and the world is justified. Such people are greater than sin. They do not solve the problem of guilt. But, in their lives, they bear it away. They are the people who take away the sins of the world.

The gospel has preserved the name of one of those men who was called in this way. What we meet in the long lines of people, we recognize in one man in that line. What takes place and is worthy of our faith in countless people on earth, we encounter in this one man on earth, who became so deeply involved in this whole guilty world that he became, in Paul's words, sin. He is the man of whom we say, in the table prayer during the celebration of the Eucharist, that he—together with countless other people—is the forgiveness of all sins.

About Psalm 80

TEXT

Shepherd of Israel, hear our prayer.
You, leading Joseph like a flock,
you, enthroned on the winged animals,
guide and blessing of Benjamin,
God of Ephraim and Manasseh,
show your glory for us to see,
stir up your power and come to our rescue.

Be here among us,
light in the midst of us,
be our saviour,
bring us to life.

O Lord, God of the powers, how long yet
will you turn angrily away when we pray?
We have had to eat the bread of tears,
a flood of tears you made us drink.
We are the plaything of our neighbors,
we are the laughing-stock of our enemies.

God of the powers,
light in the midst of us,
be our saviour,
bring us to life.

There was a vine in the land of Egypt,
with tender care you dug it out;
then you drove away other nations
in order to plant it in their land.
You tilled the soil to make it grow,
to let it take root in every place
and spread itself over all the country—
and with its shadow it covers the mountains,
and with its twigs the divine cedars;
it stretches its branches out to the sea,
its tendrils down to the great River.

Why, then, were its fences destroyed?
Why can every passer-by
plunder and loot it, why do the boars
break loose from the forest to trample it down,
why are the vermin stripping it bare?

God of the powers,
be our saviour,
be here among us,
bring us to life.

From your heaven look down on this vine,
go out, recover it, cherish the stock
which you planted with your own hand.
May those who once burnt it like firewood
be consumed in the fire of your anger.

But never again take away your hand,
away from the one whom you have chosen,
away from Man, the son of your mercy.

We will never turn from you again.
Make us new and we call your Name:

God of the powers,
be here among us,
light in the midst of us,
bring us to life.

COMMENTARY

"To the tune of the lilies. A testimony of Asaph. A psalm for the liturgical service."

This is what is written above this song in the Hebrew manuscripts, as a kind of direction for performance.

"In the silence of the night. Out of the depths. After he had been drinking for nine days on end, but you could not tell. A song while he was going through the darkness. For the conductor of the orchestra. A night song. A song of surrender, because I am waiting for you, and you alone, O Eternal One."

This is how Gerard Kornelis van het Reve begins one of his letters.

From the depths. Around death. For people who want to believe, but who do not know how. So as not to have to be completely silent. Be here among us. So as not to be alone.

Those words could be written above our church services and above the songs we sing in church.

Psalm 80 is to be sung. Possibly not "to the tune of the lilies," but certainly, we may hope, in such a way that people of today are able to enter into the singing and breathe and call with that testimony of a certain Asaph, to whom this song is attributed.

It says, a testimony of Asaph. It is therefore not an argument, a treatise, but a cry from the heart, a piece of your own body, a song. Asaph was a senior choirmaster, a conductor, a composer and, somewhere in the Bible, he was called a prophet. He took part in services in the temple at Jerusalem.

His name is derived from a word that means something like "a collector." His fate, his call, his task—they are all implied in that name. He had to collect the feelings of many people into one song. He had to collect a whole people's experiences of faith and of life into one testimony and the misery of countless men and women into one lament.

This psalm was made from faith and misery:

Shepherd of Israel, hear our prayer.
You, leading Joseph like a flock,
you, enthroned on the winged animals,
guide and blessing of Benjamin,
God of Ephraim and Manasseh . . .

People's names are named to remind God who he is and that he must keep his word, the word that he has given—

God, remember this man and that man and do for us, for me, what you have done for them.

This is how the psalms pray, and that is how a Jew prays, even now: "Then you were God for our fathers, for Abraham, Isaac and Jacob and all those others; now you will be God for us."

The meaning of God's name is included in names of people—what he does and who he is.

Israel had a preference for names in which a person was related to God, in which God's promise to that person was expressed. Joseph means God will perpetuate his faithfulness in you. Benjamin means son of God's right hand. Ephraim means God will make you fertile. Manasseh means God will make you forget all your sorrow. John means God will be gracious to you. Jesus means God will save. God becomes public in people's names. He expresses himself and makes himself known in human history. People make him credible —God of John XXIII, God of Daniel Berrigan, God of that man without a name who simply does justice somewhere.

Joseph, Benjamin, Ephraim, Manasseh—those names evoke a past time of salvation.

Joseph and Benjamin, the favorite children of Jacob; Ephraim and Manasseh, the sons of Joseph, born in Egypt and accepted by Jacob as his own children. Here they stand for the whole people of Israel, which was delivered from Egypt and led like a flock through the desert to an oasis of green, as Psalm 23 says: "My shepherd is the Lord, I shall never want for anything."

Psalm 80 was composed centuries and centuries after that exodus, that hour of birth, that time of grace—about 730 before Christ. Israel was a powerless and corrupt little kingdom, ruled by worthless kings and internally divided into a northern and a southern kingdom, rather like present-day Belgium. And like all little states throughout history, like Laos and Vietnam today, it was jammed in between great power blocks.

The Assyrians were at the frontiers. A few years later they were to lead the population of the northern kingdom away into exile. In a temple which might be destroyed at any moment, the cry of distress was heard:

Shepherd of Israel, hear our prayer,
show your glory for us to see,
stir up your power and come to our rescue.

Then the community joined in with the refrain:

Be here among us,
light in the midst of us,
be our saviour,
bring us to life.

It was raving, of course, asking for the impossible, wanting the absurd. A last resort, not really knowing any more what you are saying, because no one in Israel could see God's glory without dying. It was praying for death, praying to be allowed to depart, like Elijah praying under the broom bush in the desert to be set free and to go to God himself. It was mysticism—wanting to be released and to be with Jesus Christ in God.

"Be here among us," a temple full of people called, as

though it were even possible. These words are the beginning and the passionate heart of every psalm, of every prayer, of all singing.

The Rabbi Pinhas—one of the leaders of Hassidism, that school of Jewish piety which began two and a half centuries ago in the ghettos of Eastern Europe and in which the most profound inspiration of Israel lived again—would have said: "If we could truly sing, God, we should not allow you to remain there in the heights, but bring you with our songs into this world. Then all suffering would be silenced."

Anyone who thinks that that is nonsense ought simply to join in the singing and his suffering will perhaps be silenced, at least for a few moments.

Two words characterize the style of this psalm, the freedom, almost the abandon of every Jewish prayer—"how long yet" and "why."

These are words which we usually do not venture to utter when we are praying and which we are hardly able to reconcile with what we call "our faith."

"How long yet will you turn angrily away? How long must we still wait for you?" is the cry of another psalm.

"How long yet"—you call that out because you are tired of waiting so long, because you are suffering from time. Time is impossible sometimes—you cannot kill it, you cannot get through it. Grief will not wear off, so it seems at times. A hole will not simply close up. Time crawls, we say. How long yet.

"Why"—you call that out because you are suffering from senselessness. It is just not true that everything has a meaning. "Why have you abandoned me?" a psalm says, and Jesus says to his God. Why and how long yet am I to be destroyed, somebody like Job calls out, somebody in Southeast Asia, somebody in the Middle East. It is not possible to point to any meaning. There is no answer to the question.

There was a vine in the land of Egypt,
with tender care you dug it out.
You tilled the soil to make it grow,
to let it take root in every place.
It stretches its branches out to the sea,
its tendrils down to the great River.
Why, then, were its fences destroyed?
Why can every passer-by
plunder and loot it,
why are the vermin stripping it bare?

A dream, a vision of grace and the absence of grace—a people, a man, like a favorite plant, cherished and extending as far as the great River, in other words, the Euphrates, the river forming the boundary of paradise. And then, destruction. In this vision of the destroyed vine, Israel recognized her own fate and we recognize the fate of—of how many people? I recognize death itself, that moment which cannot be calculated and when everyone is homeless and meaningless, without a fence and without shelter. A body is suddenly broken down, an illusion is suddenly stripped bare, an intuitive or carefully built-up plan is suddenly ruined, someone can no longer carry on, cannot hold his own any more, against his loneliness, against life, and the only thing that cannot happen happens. Is it something like that, perhaps? And then "every passer-by" comes along and he knows what

to do—he takes it into his own hands. Then the vermin come
and strip it bare.

The puzzle, the mystery of this psalm, and of the whole
of Israel's faith, is that this vine stripped bare, this man
plundered and looted, is called the "son of God's mercy."

From your heaven look down on this vine,
and never again take away your hand,
away from the one whom you have chosen,
away from Man, the son of your mercy.

For what purpose is a man like this chosen? He is chosen
to be greater than fate. To raise up his eyes and to go on
living, whatever it may cost him, however insignificant he
may be, without bitterness and hatred.

To be a man without illusions and no longer protected by
everything that men use to protect themselves, such as optimism, ambition, convictions and lies. To have only one refuge
—the truth.

How many people live like that? That is not the question
that we should ask. Perhaps we ourselves are chosen, at a
moment which cannot be calculated in advance, to live like
that, to be greater than the fate that strikes us.

What was lived in Israel by a small remnant, a handful of
people, what is still lived in this world, anonymously and
unseen, namely, that plundered and belittle people can be
great, was seen by the gospel in him who is called the Son
of Man, the Son of God. In Jesus of Nazareth, delivered up
and belittled in the hands of men, a worm and not a man,

a vine stripped bare, poured out like water and broken like
bread. Then, the gospel tells us (in one of its resurrection
stories, that story about the transfiguration on Mount Tabor),
the heavens opened above him, light shines out through his
skin and a voice sounds from heaven: this is the son of
my mercy.

PRAYER

*In the celebration of the Eucharist
the text which follows might serve
as a table prayer.
If Psalm 80 is sung antiphonally
by the choir and the people,
the one who is leading the worship
begins by saying:*

Why are you not here,
not everywhere on earth, God,
like a healing hand,
like a liberating word,
like a light that points to new ways?
Then we would come to life again—
the wilderness would become habitable,
the desert would bear fruit,
rocks would change into springs
and stones into water.
What is impossible now
would become possible.
There would be a city of peace,
a new earth.
How long must we still wait for you?

We who are your people,
made by you, led and blessed by you
and by no other God,
we who are simply people
and who pray to you,
somewhere between birth and death,
at this moment of our lives—
we remind you
that you promised to be faithful to us
for ever and ever
and that you would never deny
the work of your hands.
We remind you
of what you have done to people
since the earliest times—
of what you did
to Abraham, Isaac and Jacob,
to your prophets, Moses and Elijah,
to David, your king,
whom you planted like a vine,
and above all to Jesus of Nazareth,
who came to carry out your will,
whom you called and chose
to be a man to the very end,
who accomplished everything
and became our servant,
who is our Lord and master,
our guide to life,
our way and our truth.

On the evening before his death,
as a sign of the spirit which filled him,

he took bread in his hands and broke it
and gave it to his disciples
with these words:
take and eat,
this is my body for you.
Do this in memory of me.

He also took the cup with the wine
and said:
this is the new covenant in my blood,
that is shed for this world
for the forgiveness of sins.

Remember that man, Lord God,
and do to us
what you did to him.
Go out and look for us
and come to our rescue.
Never take away your hand from us.
Open your heaven above us,
call our names,
send us your Spirit
and make us people,
through him and with him and in him,
your Son,
who lives for ever and ever.
Amen.

Today and Here and In Those Days

The script of a liturgical celebration
held in an average church
for about 1500 people
on December 24, 1967,
from half past nine until eleven o'clock in the evening.

A WORD OF INTRODUCTION

in which the facts
that set the tone for Christmas
are recalled.

The one who is to lead the worship
comes forward.
The place where he joins in the service,
that is, where he listens
when others are reading from scripture,
is not the sanctuary
but one of the pews at the front of the church.

He is dressed in an ordinary dark suit
and a grey, open cloak with wide sleeves
(a gown, something like a soutane, but less formal,
and not so hierarchical as a chasuble).

When he speaks,
as he does here at the opening of the meeting,
and later during the table prayer
and the bidding prayers,
he is not surrounded by deacon,
subdeacon and acolytes,
but stands alone,
facing those who are present.
To open the service,
he says, as soberly and as intelligibly as possible:

Recently,
a newspaper entry was awarded the prize
for the most artistic press photo of the year—
the photo captioned "Eighteen months old, eighteen months
    of hunger."

Recently,
hunger strikes have been held
in The Hague, Rome, Santa Barbara,
London, Lyons, New York.
Today and tomorrow
a group of students in Utrecht
are holding a hunger strike
in protest against
the insufficient help
given to the starving population of the world.

Our world spends
about a hundred milliard dollars each year
on armaments.
That is
about two hundred million dollars each minute.

In a street along one of the canals
in the center of Amsterdam,
an anti-Christmas chapel has been set up.
It contains burnt Christmas trees,
and a tape recorder repeats fragments
from the Vietnam tribunal.

Napalm is a simple combination
of benzine and a slow burning,
syrupy kind of petroleum.
Today, napalm is regarded
as a conventional weapon.

The tune of the opening song
is not difficult.
Everyone can sing it
as loudly as he likes.
It is called:
"This is the day you will see his glory."

Tomorrow
a hundred and eighty thousand children
will be born.
Our help is the Name of the Lord,
who made the heavens and the earth.

Today and tomorrow
there is conflict in Israel.
In Bethlehem
there are campaigns by Arabs
who want to go back to their own homes.
May peace and grace be yours
from God the Father who made us,

but not to tear each other to pieces,
and from Jesus, his Son,
and from the Holy Spirit who is in us.
We proclaim to you, full of joy:
here is your God.

OPENING SONG

An antiphonal song,
incorporating verses from Psalm 110
(as in the introit of the midnight mass
in the Roman rite);
the last verse anticipates
the visions of Isaiah
which are to be read afterwards.

This is the day you will see his glory,
here is your God.
This is the day that our saviour is born,
Christ the Lord.

God has spoken: you are my Son.
I have begotten you today.
You are king on the day of your birth.

This is the day you will see the light,
here is your God.
This is the day that our saviour is born,
Christ the Lord.

Light from light, of our own generation,
a child born for us, a son given to us.
He will be called: peace on earth.

Peace on earth for all men,
glory to God.
This is the day that our saviour is born,
Christ the Lord.

Just as the sea floor is covered with water,
so will the earth be covered with peace.
This is the day which the Lord has made.

We proclaim to you, full of joy:
here is your God.
This is the day that our saviour is born,
Christ the Lord.

A READING FROM THE VISIONS
OF THE PROPHET ISAIAH

A free selection of verses
from the poems which are collected
in the book of Isaiah.
The first fragment is taken from the 59th chapter,
the second from the 9th chapter,
the third from the 11th, 40th and 32nd chapters,
and the fourth from the 2nd and 11th chapters.

A man and a woman
should read these fragments in turn.

1.

No, God's hand is not too short to save,
and his ear is not too deaf to hear.
But the crimes of men obscure the light,

their hands are stained with blood
and their lips speak lies.
They are hatching adders' eggs
and weaving spiders' webs.
They practice violence and sow destruction.
They do not know the way of peace.

We are waiting for light, but it remains dark,
for the light of the sun, but we walk in darkness.
Like blind men we feel our way along the wall,
as uncertain as people who have no eyes.
We stumble in broad daylight,
in the prime of our lives we are like dead men.
We growl like bears
and moan like doves,
waiting for salvation.

2.

The people that walk in darkness
will see a powerful light.
On all who live in the shadow of death
a great and radiant light will shine.

You have made our happiness so great, God,
you make us laugh and rejoice
like men laughing at harvest time.

For the slave's yoke that oppressed us,
the bar across our shoulders,
the stick that beat us—
you will smash them, on your day.

The heavy, tramping boots of war,
the clothes died in blood—
these will be thrown on to the fire
and be a prey to the flames.

For a child is born for us,
a son is given to us.
The kingdom has been laid on his shoulders
and this is the name that he is given:
wonderful counsellor, strong God,
father for ever, king of peace.

3.

The spirit of the Lord will rest on him,
the spirit of wisdom and understanding,
the spirit of truth and power.
He will stand up for the poor and needy—
justice is the belt around his hips,
truthfulness is like a cloak around his shoulders.
He will be a screen against the wind,
a shelter from the rain.

Then a voice is heard:
make way for your God,
clear a path for him in the desert.
All the mountains and hills must be levelled,
every abyss must be filled in,
the hollows must become a plain,
the cliffs a fertile valley.
Then you will see the glory of God,
all flesh will see his glory.

Then your eyes will no longer be closed
and your ears will no longer be blocked.
Then he will pour his spirit for ever on us—
the wilderness will become an orchard
and all the trees will be in flower.

4.

Then all the peoples of the earth
will beat their swords into ploughshares
and their lances into sickles
to harvest the corn,
and no nation will draw its sword against another
and no one will train for battle.

Then the panther will nestle beside the kid,
the wolf and the lamb will lie down together,
the calf and the lion will graze on the same field
and a child can take them to pasture.
The infant will play at the adder's hole
and the child will put his hand into the snake's nest.

And no man will ever again cause disaster.
Just as the sea floor is covered with water,
so will the earth be covered with peace.

VERSES FROM PSALM 118

*The choir sings the text
while a flute plays the original melody
(Geneva 1551).*

The Lord has helped me in my sadness,
I called to him—he set me free.

He is my song, he brings me gladness
and, like a friend, stands up for me.
The Lord's right hand is strong to save us,
the Lord's right hand is raised up high,
and I shall sing of all he gave us,
for I shall live, I shall not die.

We sing this song to you, proclaiming
this is the day the Lord has made,
and we rejoice in it, acclaiming
you as our God, so long delayed.
Accept, O God, our glad thanksgiving,
our praise of you, whose help is sure.
Your light has risen on the living,
your love endures for evermore.

THE GOSPEL OF JESUS CHRIST ACCORDING TO LUKE

In a new translation,
sung by a cantor
to a Gregorian melody.

In those days
an order was promulgated by Caesar Augustus
that a census had to be taken
throughout the whole world.
This census took place
before Quirinus was governor of Syria.
Everyone set off to be registered,
each one in his own town.

Joseph too set off,
and since he was of David's house and lineage,
he went from the town of Nazareth in Galilee
up to Judaea,
to Bethlehem, the town of David,
to be registered there,
together with Mary, his wife, who was with child.

And while they were staying in Bethlehem,
the time came for her to have her child.
She brought a son into the world,
her first-born,
wrapped him in swaddling clothes
and laid him in a manger,
because there was no room for them at the inn.

Now there were shepherds near-by;
that night, they were out in the fields,
watching over their flocks.
Suddenly an angel of the Lord stood before them
and the glory of the Lord shone around them
and they were filled with fear.
But the angel spoke to them:
do not be afraid,
because I bring you news of great joy
intended for all the people.
Today a saviour is born for you
in the town of David.
His name is Christ the Lord.
And this will be a sign for you:
you will find a new-born baby,
wrapped in swaddling clothes
and lying in a manger.

And suddenly the angel was surrounded
by a host of heavenly powers,
praising God and singing:

> *The choir strikes up*
> *and all join in.*

Glory to God in the highest
and peace on earth to all people
of good will.

ADDRESS

If I sing those words, then everything is all right—it is a
vision, a desire, a dream. When I am singing, I am carried
along, I am lifted up above the questions that are buzzing
around in my head—what is peace, who is peace, who is God?
But if I have to say the words as they are printed, say them
to you—"Peace on earth, glory to God, here is your God"—
they are suddenly a long way away and almost impossible to
understand.

We should not think of ourselves as being greater than we
are. We are, here in this church tonight, no greater than
we always have been, but we are people of good will. And
we are impotent—too little for the problem of world peace
and often too little, or too great, too high-handed, too stub-
born for peace in ourselves.

This Christmas service too—despite all the trouble that has
been taken to provide suitable music for it, is no more than
a little service that we can render to each other here. It is
no guarantee of anything—not even of the few days that lie

ahead, in the perhaps precarious intimacy of your own family or circle of friends.

"Today a saviour is born for you." Today is now. The vision sounds good. It is beautiful, perillously beautiful: "seeing ruins and singing of beautiful weather." Today is the reality and that has a bitter sound—once again, we have failed to achieve anything more than "a twenty-four-hour cease-fire." Sometimes you must think, sceptically and unable to escape: we shall never succeed. And there is no one in the world who is able to change everything overnight, from war to peace, from death to life, so that we may say: today everything has been made new, we have been changed into peace, we were not born in vain. "Here is your God." There are other visions which, we feel at least, come closer to reality: "Like blind men we feel our way along the wall—in the prime of our lives we are like dead men—we growl like bears and moan like doves, waiting for salvation."

We proclaim to you, full of joy: here is your God. This is the day that our saviour is born, Christ the Lord.

Saviour is the oldest name in our language for Jesus of Nazareth and saviour means rescue, cure, healing. A saviour as a child, a saviour as vulnerable, as inconspicuous and as unarmed as a child. A new-born baby cannot attack, cannot threaten, cannot kill. A baby reveals to me what the whole world, all that violent, warring "today," makes me forget. A baby calls the deepest, forgotten experiences back to me— that I am not a murderer, that I was not born to hate and kill.

Sometimes it seems to me as though the whole world is trying to persuade me to accept the law of the strongest, trying to convince me that aggression is good, that I must always be on my guard, watching out—enough to make me neurotic. But a child tells us that in the beginning it was not so. A new-born baby, that is, you shall not kill. He rescues us. He tells us that we are not murderers, we helmeted and masked men who just talk, we men with our imperious gaze and our mortal fear of losing, turning our eyes fearfully away from almost every other man to avoid meeting his eyes. Yet we are good enough, all the same, to bring a child into the world, to look at him and to make him live. Christmas is not a man, not a hero, not a shattering impression, but a child—a child too little to cry out and protest against.

Is there any way out of this impossible war, any way that leads to an impossible peace? Can it happen in people? Here is your God. Nothing spectacular is taking place today. No extra session in the legislature, no sudden decision to devote two per cent of the gross national product to aid the developing countries. No voice heard throughout the world, penetrating these walls and calling: light, and there is light; peace, and there is peace. No, that way does not exist. That God does not exist.

But he does exist, he does happen in people who have become so little, so inconspicuous and so defenseless themselves that they no longer attack, no longer bite back and no longer accuse, people who are no longer able to do what leads to war. There is no other story about God today—he happens in people who want to be so little that they are no longer able to kill. They follow, in themselves, the lonely way from war to peace. They beat their weapons into something quite ordinary, into a ploughshare for tilling the soil, a spoon for ladling up food. And they no longer train for battle.

He can happen in you. I hardly dare to say this, because it is so difficult, because the meaning of your life is the most difficult thing in your life. Beating your weapons—that happens in fire. But whoever recognizes it, this vision of peace, may know that he recognizes himself, that he recognizes his own future. A vision is growing in us, it will happen, it will be made public—the wolf and the lamb will lie down together, the pitiless and the defenseless will be reconciled in us. It has been promised. It cannot be said. Perhaps it can be sung.

"In deepest night the star of morning
has heralded the infant's birth.
A child of men is born for us
and God will save us is his name."

THE SONG OF THE LORD'S APPEARANCE

In deepest night the star of morning
has heralded the infant's birth.
His coming is for us the dawning
of God's salvation here on earth.
Trust what you see, believe the vision,
lay bare your hearts to God's own word,
do not refuse the saviour's mission,
accept the message you have heard.

God has no other sign, no other
light in our darkened world to give
than this man Christ to be our brother,
a God with whom we all can live.
He has revealed to every nation
his love of man in Christ our Lord.
In him all flesh may see salvation,
and earth made new in God's own word.

The promised one of Israel's story,
the bridegroom clad in fire and light,
the morning sun in all its glory
dispelling darkness and the night,
has come to dwell with us for ever,
uniting us in peace and love,
and in his body we need never
be parted from our God above.

INTERMISSION

During which a collection may be made.

*Someone puts the plates with bread
and the cup with wine on the table.
Music is played and the people
listen to it.*

*After about five minutes
the one who is leading the worship
goes up to the table,
stands behind it
and prays.*

THE TABLE PRAYER

Before we speak
you have already heard us.
You are the only one, our God.
Before we go to you
you are already near to us,
in us and above us,
eternal and unseen.
You live in us,
you, the only one, our God.
We admire you
because you dare to be with us here.
We thank you
because you care for us,
because people are not too lowly for you.

But in that case you will also listen to us
and allow us to come to you
and approve of our praying to you,
again and again
and once more on this night,
and always for the same thing—
for peace.
What would be left
of that covenant between you and men
if there were no justice
here on earth, between men?
We remind you
of your great acts of salvation and mercy,
of the word you once gave us,
of everything you promised and made true
in Jesus of Nazareth, the son of men,

whom you saved from death
and whom you made peace.

We keep you to that word,
Lord God,
we keep you to him.
Do to us what you did to him.
For why him and not us?
Why him living with you
and us here, given up to ourselves?

Make us turn inwards and repent,
call our names,
for you are the only one, our God.
Make us people
who no longer hate,
no longer kill.
Make people of us today
if you can.

Show us, if only for a little time,
on this night, this Christmas-time,
that the impossible is possible,
that we, however old and great we may be,
can become little and be born again,
that it can happen—peace on earth,
that fear can be allayed,
hunger appeased,
justice done,
bread broken and joy shared
between men.
This is, after all, what your prophets have foretold.
Hasten the time
and establish your future.

This is, after all, what he has already done for us—
he was, and is, a child of men
who, on the night before his suffering and death,
took bread in his hands,
broke it and gave it to his disciples
with these words:
take and eat,
my body for you.
Do this in memory of me.

He also took the cup,
and, giving thanks to you, said:
this cup is the new covenant in my blood,
shed for you and for all men
for the forgiveness of sins.
Every time you drink this cup,
you will do it in memory of me.

> *The celebrant, choir and people*
> *now sing the following hymn*
> *antiphonally.*
> *It is taken from the Didache.*

Whenever we eat of this bread
and drink from this cup,
we proclaim the death of the Lord
until he comes.

Blessed is he who comes in the name of the Lord,
Jesus Messiah.
Come to our rescue,
O Son of David.

Blessed are you, O Lord God, our Father,
for the sake of David, the holy vine,
in which you have let us share
through Jesus, your servant.

To you alone is all honor due,
for ever.

Blessed are you for all wisdom and all life,
in which you have let us share
through Jesus, your servant.

To you alone is all honor due,
for ever.

Just as the bread that we break
was sown as seed in the ground
and was gathered together and was made one,
so bring us together from far and wide
into the kingdom of your peace.

To you alone is all honor due,
for ever.

So we pray to you with the words
which Jesus, your Son, has given us:

Our Father, who art in heaven,
hallowed be thy name.
Thy kingdom come.
Thy will be done,
on earth, as it is in heaven.
Give us this day our daily bread,

and forgive us our trespasses,
as we forgive those who trespass against us,
and lead us not into temptation,
but deliver us from evil. Amen.

> *The bread is then broken and shared.*
> *After that, the cup is handed round*
> *in a smaller circle*
> *representative of the people*
> *who meanwhile, together with the choir,*
> *sing:*

THE SONG OF THE NEW GOD

Though filled with expectation,
we had not yet seen you.
Now you are our salvation,
a God who is quite new.
You live among us here,
a God, a man for others,
so far and yet so near.

Your suffering and glory,
your free, redeeming word,
a name, an ancient story
are all that we have heard.
Now we no longer wait,
for you have come among us
to share our human fate.

Born in a dusty manger,
your only place on earth.
God's word and yet no stranger,

our life is in your birth.
In this poor bed you lie,
a son, a helpless baby,
a name that has to die.

BIDDING PRAYERS

These prayers are said here,
just before the dismissal,
to end the service "today and here."
After the first and second prayers,
the organ plays a short prelude
to the melody of the concluding song.

Let us pray—
and let us do even more than that—
for this world which is our world,
for everyone with whom we are associated,
for our children, our friends and those we love,
for our enemies.
Let us pray
for all people with responsibility—
both those in high positions in the world
and those who are obscure—
for all leaders of governments,
for those in authority in the churches,
for artists and scholars,
for doctors and nurses,
for mothers entrusted with the care of their families,
for those who go to the underdeveloped countries,
for all who work in the missions
and for all who are just.
You see all of us, God,

you place your hope in us
and give us the strength
to be good.

Let us pray
for the people all around us
whose lives are difficult and troubled
and whose suffering is unseen,
for those who are sad and disillusioned
and for those who can no longer find any meaning in life.
Let us also pray
for people who are alone in life,
who cannot get through the day
or find friendship anywhere.
We pray, God,
for all who are victims,
murdered people,
those who die in traffic accidents,
for children who have no parents,
for prisoners and strangers,
for refugees without a country and without a name,
Jews, Arabs, Greeks, Ambonese,
for people who live in conflict with each other
and who cannot find any solution to it,
for those who are ill without any hope of cure.
We also pray to you, God,
for our dead.
Remember their names and preserve their lives.

Let us pray
for all the special cares and problems
that have been commended to us.
For . . .

Lord God,
we ourselves are all these words,
all this time of prayer.
You know the abyss
in which we can be lost.
From the depths we are calling you, God;
on this day of your love of men
we call to you.
We are still living—
keep us alive.
We ask you this
with Jesus, your Son.

DISMISSAL AND BLESSING

Go now, all of you, in peace
to the place
where God has given you responsibility
and he himself will bless you,
the Father, the Son and the Holy Spirit.

The service concludes with

THE SONG "NOW WE BID YOU WELCOME"

Now we bid you welcome, Jesus our dear Lord;
You come among your people as God's own word.
Stay with us and save us—we shall count ourselves most blessed.
Here on earth no stranger, you are our welcome guest.
Kyrieleis!

Christe Kyrieleison—this is our refrain.
In Mary's happy childbirth there was no pain.
Jesus was born for us on this joyful Christmas night;
in this world of darkness he came to bring us light.
Kyrieleis!

In the fields the shepherds could not yet rejoice,
but then they saw the angel and heard his voice:
hurry now to Bethlehem and this will be your sign—
you will find the baby of royal David's line.
Kyrieleis!

Then the wise men came there, following the star;
they were not yet God's people, but from afar.
Kneeling down in adoration, so we have been told,
they gave Jesus treasures—myrrh, frankincense and gold.
Kyrieleis!*

* The author's original texts of most of the songs in this book are, of
course, contemporary in thought and language. This song, however, "Nu
zijt wellekome," is a very old Dutch carol. No attempt has been made
here to reproduce its flavor in "late medieval" English. —Translator.

The Tent of Meeting

Everything, amost everything that people experience in the way of joy and sadness comes out in words and cries, in language and sign.

"Life" must be discussed in language. It must be played over afterwards and before in words, it must be expressed in images and acted out and laughed at. We have to get rid of it. People want to see and hear who we are—this is why there is so much passionate writing, filming and singing going on all the time in such a variety of keys. Strip cartoons and plays, newspapers and news services, waves of publicity—there is no end to man's need for expression and communication, however disorientated and nerve-racking it may be. Frantic attempts to find recognition as a person and to find one's direction in life—who are you, we human beings, look at me, this is me, the family of men, behold the man. Finding one's direction—setting the compass, pointing it, seeking information and guidance, groping towards the horizon, the limits of the earth, the dawn.

"If we are really to find our direction, we need an art which will make us human beings recognize the sorrow and the joy of our humanity in the midst of the civilization of this world" (Fokke Sierksma).

There are houses everywehere for this art—points of contact, theatres, cinemas, tents of meeting, places and halls where we can see and hear. After all, our eyes are never tired of seeing and our ears can never hear too much. Everywhere in the world and even now, people still like to get together in a circle round a platform and there is always someone with something to say who will get up on a cart or a chair or build a stage—Pete Seeger, Yevtuchenko or Lurelei. What would happen if all this ceased?

In between all these tents of meeting, there are still houses where what happened once in Israel and what has been described in the writings of Israel, known as the Bible, from Abraham down to Jesus of Nazareth and his followers, is played and handed down in story and song. Houses where people get together to be instructed in their lives by the stories and songs of Israel about God and man, love and death, peace and justice, to find recognition and direction in life in these images and likenesses.

Houses built around the Bible, houses where that book is played and sung, proclaimed in language and sign, houses where it can be understood and experienced with a "voice of singing," as the prophet Isaiah put it.

Everything that is described in the Bible, "for our instruction" and to give us direction, in dead letters and in printed letters, becomes fascinating, astonishing and exalting when it is done—spoken aloud, called out aloud, prayed, doubted and questioned aloud and acclaimed. The Bible is invocation, prophecy and applause. It is a story that has to be told by living voices and heard rather than read.

Reading on my own, I am still lonely and isolated—either I understand the faith of Israel or I do not. Reading on my own, I am still "outside" and "opposite." But as soon as the book is set free by singing from the printed letters and brought to life, as soon as it goes back to its source—the living meeting—and once again becomes what it was before—a witness of living voices—then I am carried away by it and united to it. Then it becomes my faith and my history and I rise above pure understanding or lack of understanding and reach hearing and knowledge. Then I myself become Israel—behold the man, you are that man, I am that man.

The Bible played and sung in a variety of keys—that is the art known as "liturgy."

There are houses everywhere for this art, tents of meeting, churches.

The church does not exist. Just as "man" does not exist. There are only men, people, quite concrete, quite different from each other, this man or woman next to me. And there is a movement afoot among people that is called "faith," a way, broad or narrow, two thousand or four thousand years old, which runs through history to the point where we are now. An event, visible here and there in this world, which has been called, in ancient terms, the "community of God" and, in some of the books of the New Testament, in speculative and visionary language the "body of Christ."

Jerusalem in the years 35–40—Jesus of Nazareth is proclaimed and, in that preaching, the name of God is once again made meaningful and valid. It once again arouses faith and calls people together—"on one day, about three thousand people joined." That word of proclamation reproduced itself in people's thinking and acting together and inspired them to create new forms of life. We read of the results of this in the Acts of the Apostles: "Those who had accepted faith were of one heart and soul. No one called anything that he had his own property. Everything they possessed was held in common and none of them ever went in need." Vague terms, but words that have continued to fascinate us up to the present time, words which characterize the way of life of those who follow Jesus. Not a blueprint for the building up of a new society, but a parable which suggests that the impossible is sometimes possible.

Of course, these people of Jesus met together "in some house" to read aloud to each other from the scriptures, to "persist in prayer and the breaking of bread." Where there are language and sign in which this new life with each other is expressed and confirmed, there is liturgy.

"The" Church is too much to call by one name and it is above all too much to cope with. In ordinary conversation, the most contradictory facts and phenomena are called "the" Church (and "Christianity")—all kinds of moral principles and religious practices and the most unselfish service and love of poor and rejected people, both a clannish group of Roman prelates and a Francis of Assissi, both purely human activities and so-called "divine" institutions. "The" Church is a concept which can neither be understood nor managed. "A" church is some house where the art of the liturgy is carried out as a service to people who, "in the midst of the civilization of this world," want to try to recognize the sorrow and the joy of their humanity and the extent of their solidarity with

each other in the words of Israel and who try to find their
direction in life in the experience of life and the conjecture
of God's existence that grew up and was preserved in Israel.
Liturgy is a service to people who are trying to believe.

Liturgy used always to be above all a service in honor and
worship of God.

Sacred liturgy, an act of adoration, one of the most sublime
tasks of the Church. The directions according to which one
had to "appear" in the presence of God and "enter" the sacred
place were in themselves sacred. The liturgical vessels were
sacred and the drain down which the sacred remains of the
sacrifice were flushed was also sacred. Liturgy had no need
to be conducted in a language which people could understand—it could be better performed in forms which could
not be understood, which alienated people and cast a beautiful spell on them, in gestures which were strictly stylized.
Liturgy was cultivated in select companies, manipulated by
a celibate élite. As if the depths of God's inaccessible light
and of his sublimity were most effectively suggested in this
way.

In the long run, the celebration of the liturgy became, for
the vast majority of believers, kneeling or standing in silence
and inside oneself joining in a little in ancient incomprehensible sounds and beautiful foreign melodies and being a
humble spectator at a ceremony that was regulated down to
the smallest and most absurd details—the priest must keep
his thumb and forefinger firmly pressed together after the
words of consecration, must kiss the altar stone with the
sacred relics over which two linen cloths must be laid with
five crosses embroidered on them, which means that . . .

About one thing there can be no doubt whatever—the humility of the millions of people who have, throughout time, allowed themselves to be carried away by such a strange, fascinating event.

For some years now, however, another kind of church service has been developing, a service not in the first place in honor and worship of God, but a service of proclamation in which people come together to prove to each other the ministry of the word. In this kind of meeting, those who in one way or another "go before" the others in the service do not behave like members of a royal court, do not move about with their hands folded and their eyes cast down, do not isolate themselves in strange garments, in facial expressions, in gestures, inflections of the voice and attitudes of prayer —all the aspects of the manner that the ministers of the sacred in every religion have to acquire. No, in this other kind of service, everything that is done is directed towards giving the word its full power of expression and making scripture intelligible. And those who come to this kind of service, not to "assist at" anything (such as a sacrifice), but to take part in an act of witness, a game of singing and listening, will take most notice of those forms which make them most disposed to be converted and to respond.

A church in Amsterdam or somewhere else. On Sunday morning. A service to people who are trying to believe, who believe somehow or other—a little bit or very much, with scepticism, very piously, unstably, sentimentally, progressively. Some of those who come are completely at a loss as far as their own Church denomination is concerned. There are those who can no longer hear or understand the word God.

Others come only to be strengthened in their old, familiar ways and convictions, to be assured that the past was right. It is impossible to estimate precisely why these people still come and with what private thoughts and expectations or because of what fears. But in any case everyone is welcome and everyone is treated as a guest. And everyone who comes wants to join in with all the others who have also come, whether they sniff or whether they bellow during the singing.

Various people have tasks on Sunday morning in a tent of meeting like this. There is not just one minister, one player (with two or more altar servers like pages around him). There is not simply one spokesman, who may perhaps speak unintelligibly or have a boring voice and nothing much to say. The parts are shared—there is a choir to lead the people and inspire them in the singing, there may be a singer, a soloist or cantor, there are readers and musicians, there is someone who preaches—the priest on the spot or someone else among the community who is more gifted or more called to preach —and someone else who says the eucharistic table prayer in the name of everyone present.

There is alternation of voices, combination of functions, variation of expression and sound. There are various ways of speaking—narrative, imploring, vociferous and stirring, sober and communicative. A bidding prayer is said differently from a reading of the gospel and the blessing sounds different from the opening address.

But what goes much farther than the spoken word is everything that is sung. The speaking voice interprets and narrows down human experience, the song (for one voice, for several voices, sung in verses or antiphonally, short as a cry or long-winded as a hymn) is broader and goes deeper. A sermon may perhaps be didactic, dogmatic, polemical or ethical. But the song is more guileless, joyful, effective and human than any way of speaking. A song may be admonitory, instructive and catechetic, but if it is good it is always more than this. The sung word is the very heart of the liturgy.

Of course no books are given out or sold at the beginning of a service like this, nobody brings a missal in which everything that is said or sung can be at the same time followed or into which it is possible to retreat in order to say one's "private" prayers. Never again will there be missals at this sort of service, with one form of mass for every Sunday of the year and exactly the same text for every place in the world, texts composed by the liturgical commission in Rome. The only printed book used in the service is one containing songs—always new songs. All the rest is oral tradition, hearing something said or sung.

Everyone can sing and everyone's voice is good enough. Singing is discovered and invented, it is born at times when there is no other possible way for people to express themselves —at a grave, for example, where four or five people with untrained, clumsy voices sing words that are greater and smaller than their faith and their experience: "no one lives for himself, no one dies for himself."

Singing is becoming part of a greater whole, joining in, agreeing with many other people, using words which you cannot make true if you sing them alone, but which you can only venture to sing together with others. With all my doubts, I am really in my proper place in a community that sings, I am protected by a healthy anonymity. The song that is sung

together is often a legitimate excuse for my personal impotence
as a believer.

The secret of singing is that you cannot help doing it.
Singing is what happens in one of the stories that the Argen-
tinian writer Julio Cortázar has written about the cronopios,
the famas and the esperanzas, fantastic beings to whom
nothing human is alien.

When the cronopios sing their favorite songs, they become
so enthusiastic that they are often run over by lorries or
knocked down by cyclists or they fall out of the window and
lose what they had in their pockets, even the calendar. When
a cronopio sings, the esperanzas and the famas come and
listen although they do not really understand why the cronopios are so carried away and find it a little offensive. In the
center of the circle, the cronopio lifts up his arms as though
he had to hold up the sun, as though the sky were a tray
and the sun the head of John the Baptist, so that the cronopio's song is the naked Salomé, who dances before the
famas and esperanzas who stand there with their mouths
open and wonder whether the priest . . . whether it is becoming or proper . . . But, because they are at heart good
(famas are good and esperanzas are stupid), they clap the
cronopio, who recovers with a start, looks around and begins
to clap himself, the rogue.

A tent of meeting is a place where people sing with others.
In our world there are very few other places where this
happens.

Of course there is an order of service, a flexible and open
pattern which gives direction to the meeting and a basic
structure to the event of proclamation. We do not just do

something, but follow the broad outline of all the great liturgies in history. But we do not feel that we are bound to include all the elements, most of them questionable, which have become attached to that basic structure throughout the course of history. For example, the detailed mutual confession of guilt (the "Confiteor") with which almost all church services, Catholic or Protestant, begin, the prayers at the offertory and the "Lord, I am not worthy" said three times before going to communion.

The original pattern of the Christian liturgy and of the Jewish service in the synagogue from which the Christian service developed is a succession of reading from the scriptures, psalm and prayer—proclamation, praise and petition.

We begin by singing our way into the scriptures. We gradually warm up to it, gather our hearts and voices together and, by singing with each other, become a community that is ready to listen. Then comes the word, read aloud, proclaimed and "interpreted." Our response to the word is twofold—we sing a song in which we tune ourselves in to what we have heard and make it our own by singing, and we say the bidding prayers, in which we become the whole world and everyone in it and express in many different questions this one petition—you who will come to make all things new, make us justice and peace.

Within this basic order of service the theme of proclamation is elaborated, played on and varied—by free association, not so much by reasoning, demonstration or discursive thought, but by suggestion and poetic understanding, like the scriptures themselves. Liturgy is a free collection of images and likenesses Words evoke other words—the complaint of the bride looking for her lover (in the fifth chapter of the Song of Songs), the "song of the beloved," evokes the passage from John's gospel about Mary Magdalen looking for Jesus of Nazareth in the garden on Easter morning. Visions merge with each other—the garden of the resurrection becomes the garden of the story of creation where a man and a woman find each other and call each other by name. The mysterious links in the Bible itself between one story and another are brought to light—Moses going up the mountain to be there with God and speak with him, eye to eye, man to man, and Jesus going up the mountain, going into heaven to be "there" in the concealment of God.

In a "liturgical formula," we proclaim and hear the faith of Israel—the people who dared to do the impossible, going through the sea, living through death. We read, for instance, from the book of Exodus, that epic of the people's journey through the water of death, the Red Sea. Then we sing Psalm 114, that song about the sea taking to flight, the mountains jumping like rams, like lambs—images for what cannot exist—and about a God who does what is impossible—changing rocks into springs and pools, stones into water. Then we read again in scripture and hear in the gospel how Jesus of Nazareth (in whom the earliest Christian community believed that Israel's mystery was revealed and her destiny fulfilled) walked over the water and trod death underfoot and is the living, the saved lord of water and death and all the powers that threaten us. This is the right place to sing Psalm 46, with its theme of the water, of death and of God:

and let the water foam and rage,
assault the cliffs to set them rocking—
he is for us the God of the powers.

When we read and sing about God and Jesus in this way the covenant between the two of them—they are called by one and the same name and at the same time—is evoked more clearly, more powerfully and with greater purity than it is in such traditional theological terms as God-man, Christ's divinity and the second Person of the Holy Trinity.

In the scriptures water is not only an image and likeness of death—it is also an image and likeness of life. In all the myths of mankind water is both the threat of death and the origin of life, the grave and the womb. Israel was born again of the water of the sea; in John's gospel we read about being born of water and the Spirit; the man born blind, whom Jesus saw "in passing," washed himself in the water of the Pool of Siloam and lived again; John speaks of a source of living water rising up in him who believes, the Holy Spirit. The same Psalm 46 evokes the vision of a stream of living water that branches out "through the city of the Most High. There he lives—it will stand firm."

This city, John tells us in his apocalyptic visions (in imitation of the prophet Ezekiel), this tent of God in the midst of people, is a bride for her husband, Eve for Adam, new creation, genesis completed, man become man.

A purely spoken liturgy—address, argument and catechesis —is not able to reproduce the full meaning and expressiveness of these images and likenesses, the experince of faith and the human existential experience which are incorporatd in them, so effectively and so compellingly as a sung liturgy, which can suggest to us in the songs we sing and the stories we hear that all of this is also still true.

Since time immemorial, the scriptural service has been followed in the Christian liturgy by the service of the table, the "breaking of the bread." A sign is presented in which the meaning of the words appears.

In scripture reading, song and prayer, it is proclaimed to all who are gathered round the table that they are the "body of Christ," that they are called to become justice and peace, as he was, bread and strength for this world. In the breaking and distribution of the bread, that most human of all rites, this is announced once again to the assembled people. They come forward with their hands open to receive the meaning of their existence, their "name" and, as Augustine put it, "they say amen to their own mystery." In the gospel, the name of Jesus is handed to us—bread for the life of this world is what he is called there, servant, a "man for others." In the sign of the Eucharist, we receive his name, recognize and accept physically, with our hands, that he became bread and strength for this world—that he gave himself to the end, as every eucharistic prayer says, and that only this attitude is our salvation.

Liturgy is proclamation in language and sign, the action added to the word. Word and gesture are more effective as proclamation than the word alone. The gesture completes and confirms. It is word in action. In theological language this is called "sacrament."

The sacrament fulfills a function within the proclamation. It does not work of itself, but does what a word does and that can be a great deal or very little. A child who is baptized does not suddenly become quite different from an unbaptized child, just as a "civil" marriage is no less a marriage than one solemnized by the Church, and a good life with one's fellow men is not dependent on taking part in a celebration of the Eucharist. Who could be so bold as to make such a claim? A sacrament can never be an imperative, as in most religions in which a rite is a magic obligation which is accomplished, whatever happens, at fixed times.

Language and sign, word and sacrament—these are together a free offer to be recognized. An eloquent gesture, a meaningful word in which we act out our faith for each other. On the evening before Easter we distribute light to each other, we play with fire and, in that game, we remember and know that we are called to set light to and inspire each other and that we can and should hand on, from person to person, the light that is available in this universe. A gesture of resurrection, a sign of life. When parents part with their child at a baptism and give him to others, they are anticipating, in a sense gambling on the future and giving their consent to what they promise in words—that they will remain faithful to and respect their child, yet leave him free to go wherever he may go, always remembering that he is born of God. When two people put a ring on each other's fingers on their wedding day, this rite means that they recognize and accept each other in the presence of everyone and promise to be faithful to each other, but of course this gesture is in no sense a guarantee for the future. When we hand on to each other a cup with wine in the celebration of the Eucharist, what we are doing is acting out our desire to share our inspiration and joy, our blood with each other—the sweet, intoxicating and passionate part of our life just as much as what is necessary, the bread— and in that gesture we bear witness to our faith that Jesus of Nazareth, and in him God himself, gave himself to be drunk as wine, as water and fire: "I am the vine," "This is my blood." But all these gestures of faith and consent are only meaningful and intelligible within the framework of the proclaimed word. The word is the soul and the sense of the gestures—*verbum est forma sacramenti,* as Thomas Aquinas said long ago—just as the "sacramental" gesture can bring the word of proclamation vividly to life and give it an intensity of communication which is usually denied to the word alone.

Liturgical rites like breaking bread, distributing light and handing on wine are simple gestures which reveal the original intention and form of our existence. They are completely clear and unambiguous.

The reality of our life is complicated—for the most part political, involved, partly lies, tiresome little games. I have to live with all that, all those compromises and untruths, so much which makes me no longer myself, no longer free.

But everywhere there is a hunger for simplicity, or gestures which reveal and declare the deepest, the truest reality and in which we can honestly confess what we really are and what we want to be. Sharing something with each other, holding up your hand and then handing on what you have received —these are such gestures, meaningful and as guileless as parables.

Liturgical rites are prophecy enacted. They hold up feelings before me, a depth and directness of living that I am not yet able to cope with. Joining in a rite of this kind is being amenable to the future, being responsive to what has still to come. We—people who move about parallel to each other without touching, like strangers, full of aggressiveness and hatred—we present this sign of our faith that it may some time perhaps be different. I eat and drink together with my brother, anonymous and silent, in a stylized ritual that transcends the personal level, even before I have been able to be

reconciled with him. This is not hypocristy, but a confession
of guilt and an inner commitment to the possibility that there
may some time be peace between us.

The liturgy gives us forms of expression when we ourselves are often formless and uninspired. Forms in which we
can be together with many other people, very contrasting and
very differently motivated. Forms in which excessive personal
emotion or spontaneous individual impulses are regulated
and become generally recognizable.

Taking part in the liturgy is a way of associating with each
other—not in a loud-mouthed, mocking, brusk or demanding
way, but a way in which we dare to look at each other and
speak to each other in the light of what really inspires us. It
is also a way of associating with quite ordinary things—with
someone else's work, a song for example, with your own
voice, with the money in your pocket, with food. A church
service is getting practice in the forms of association and the
style of faith. Religious practice, discipline. Acquiring the
discipline of repetition, for example. Anyone who has ever
seen and unmistakably experienced anything, a vision, a
future, is bound to go on looking for words and forms in
which he can revive that original moment just a little. He
is bound to go on persistently remembering, practicing discipline and faithfulness to keep that memory alive.

Liturgy is discipline and faithfulness against the forgetfulness of time and boredom. A church service in which what
really counts is persistence and inner recollection can never be
spectacular or popular. It can never be a stunt. It is bound to
be a dedication to values which are always being forgotten,
a practice in useless wisdom.

Liturgy is daring to use old words which we would not have thought of or found ourselves, words which have been handed down to us in an incalculably long tradition which is often dubious, words such as holy, Holy Spirit, grace.

We have no glory,
we have no name
but the name of Jesus, the Lord.
We have no glory but his cross.

Great is the mystery of our faith—
he was made public in the flesh
and justified in the Spirit
and he appeared to the angels.
He was proclaimed to the people
and he found faith here in the world
and he was taken up in glory.

If we have died with him,
then we shall also live with him.
If we hold firm, we shall reign with him,
then we shall live and reign with him.
If we deny him, he will deny us.
We may be faithless—he is faithful,
for he cannot deny himself.

We have no glory,
we have no name
but the name of Jesus, the Lord.
We have no glory but his cross.

This song, which can be used in the service of Maundy Thursday, is composed of fragments of ancient hymns quoted

by Paul in his letters, cryptic verses, probably dating from the
time of the earliest communities of Christians.

We do not simply write off these obscure verses, but try
to enter them, grow into them. We accept them on the
authority of the past as words of our own faith and put them
into our mouths, suck them, sing their meaning, their power
of suggestion, into ourselves—or something like that. And
sometimes an incomprehensible word becomes intelligible. It
sometimes begins to work inside us, evokes our own immense
past inside us, stimulates us to consent or to protest or to both.

There are words, old words, which sometimes shed their
obscurity and become quite clear in the light of a new inter-
pretation. It was said of Jesus of Nazareth, who was called
the image and son of God, God for us, in mythical words
which can never be demythologized, that he descended from
heaven and became man. Anyone who understands this falter-
ing statement as an attempt to express God's humility and
selflessness and anyone who has ever personally witnessed
and experienced people descending sometimes from their
heavens and becoming people for others may perhaps be able
to join in singing these words.

But there are also words which never give up their secret
and their hardness, dark rocks, inexplicable fragments of faith,
such as "he was conceived by the Holy Spirit and born of the
Virgin Mary." Or a piece from a hymn about life and death
like this:

Awake from your sleep,
arise from the dead
and Christ will shine his light upon you.

Within the framework of the liturgy, these words are set
up vertically, sung in the form in which they have been

preserved and handed down to us. No concessions are made. Whoever swallows them, swallows fire. Anyone who does not want to swallow them simply keeps his mouth shut. He can if he wants to.

The scripture story about a God who wants people and how he wants them, and what this means both for the people and for himself, that message told to us in the liturgy—these are strange words. They shock and alienate us like all words in which a man is revealed to himself. Perhaps we have to go right outside ourselves and leave our ordinary, everyday words if we are to be able to understand this story as our own history.

And then this message was also written down and handed on to us in an idiom that is not our own, not European, not even Germanic, not of the twentieth century. The language of the Bible will never be our own mother tongue. We shall always go on wandering around in the Bible, rather like strangers, among the phrases, images and expressions of Israel. Although the monarchy is little more than a worn-out symbol for twentieth-century man, we still sing psalms in which God is called our king and we face the challenge of trying to understand this irreplaceable word and of experiencing it in its original meaning, the meaning which it developed in Israel. And we still sing Psalm 23—my shepherd is the Lord —even though we hardly ever see a shepherd tending sheep nowadays in our own country.

Taking part in the liturgy is wanting to know that we share the history of Israel, that the name of God came to us via Israel, that it all happened like that.

"Poetry is listening back and looking forward," the poet Remco Campert once said. This might also be a definition of liturgy. Our visions of the future are handed down to us in old words, dreams of "eternal life" and light, a blind man who sees again and is reborn, a man who becomes a man, a God who says "light" and there was light. "The sea gave up the dead who were in it and death and the underworld gave up their dead," John said in his apocalyptic vision of the future.

Our world is swarming with visions, especially frightening visions, spectres, in which the fateful tendencies and dark powers which determine our lives (automation, urbanization, armament) are magnified and made absurdly radical—1984, brave new world, the year 2000.

I imagine the future to be
manufactured of rust-proof steel

said the Dutch-American poet, Leo Vroman. And as for love:

Who longs for a faint covering
waits under a clean bell-jar
an odorless light response;

one never again groans help
and no more bleeds to death
never again dies fully.

There have not been very many poets, novelists or philosophers during the last twenty-five years who have expected anything better of the future. There have been a few who, in the wake of Teilhard de Chardin, have seen a point omega gleaming in the distance, but so remote and so abstract and impossible to imagine that it has had hardly any power to attract. Most recent writers describe a mankind planning, with intelligent hands and myopic eyes, its own downfall, a future which is against man and sacrifices man. An Alphaville like that of Jean-Luc Godard, science-fiction cities in the manner of Isaac Asimov—the ground built in, steel caverns. Or hovering on an imaginary planet where people grow very old and stay quite fit and are lonely and afraid of each other's skin and the smell of each other's bodies.

Nobody fathoms the collective anxiety, the unnamable suspicion of fatality which reduces our world to a state of neurosis. But, here and there, in a tent of meeting, people do try to evoke for each other other visions and to make such visions live and make them intelligible.

A city of peace, coming down out of heaven, in the middle of it the tree of life. And there will be no more cursing there and no night and the living God will shine his light upon us. A garden where people are, not cave-dwellers with skin like glass, but man and wife with the breath of life in their nostrils and mouths that call every creature by its name. Open, unmasked people who are not ashamed of each other.

In those days, Jesus said:
there will be signs
in the sun, moon and stars
and on earth
the people will be thrown into a panic,
bewildered by the roar of the sea,
and the powers of heaven
will be shaken.
Then they will see the Son of Man coming
in a cloud with power.
When all this begins,
stand upright,
for your redemption is at hand.

A whole universe is shaken and overturned and constellations—the illuminated track towards which erring mankind turns for orientation as to a safe compass—fall. This is a vision of disaster. Then, in the middle of that disrupted system, a new point of orientation appears—the Son of Man. Like a morning star, beside which the familiar stars and certainties fade into insignificance. No longer is our destiny, our future, written in the stars. No, we read in him, in his "glorified body," what lies ahead of us and who is waiting for us. This vision of hope has been handed down to us in the gospel that there is, in the whole cosmos, no other truth to which we have to turn than the humanity and the human form of Jesus of Nazareth. We have no one else to expect.

In the liturgy this future is proclaimed to us, this hope is played to us. We anticipate what is not yet, respond playfully to this man who is to come, play with the hope and the thought that it will happen. And playing in this way, the liturgy, as the sign and witness of this hope, is more real than reality. The liturgy has to evoke the vision and keep it open, the vision that is seen and desired by all of us who are committed to this world in politics, science, art or any other sphere. But it does even more—it plays internally on every man and woman and proclaims the way that they must all go—the way of peace and disarmament, the way of becoming man. The way which is called in Israel—in Psalm 139, for example—the way of the fathers, the eternal way. The way of Jesus of Nazareth, which leads us on towards a distance of inaccessible light.

Celebrating Birth

A game, a rite
to celebrate a casual beginning
and to remind everyone present
that he too was also born once,
for, as the gospel says,
"Do not be surprised when I say:
you must be born anew."

A "sacrament" which is above all
"administered" to the parents
and which announces to them
and illuminates for them in a sign
that their child is born "of God."

The baptist has placed chairs in a circle
around a bowl with water.
There is also a seven-armed candlestick.
If there are any little children present
they are each given a candle,
mainly in order to keep them quiet.

The baptist begins by encouraging
everyone present to join in the singing,
because not singing is not so friendly and nice.

There is always someone
who can act as cantor and lead them
and probably there is also an organ
or a guitar somewhere around.

This psalm can, for example, be sung
antiphonally:

PSALM 8

Lord, our Lord, how powerful is your Name
everywhere on earth.

You show your majesty in the heavens,
yet you open the mouths of helpless children.

Lord, our Lord, how powerful is your Name
everywhere on earth.

If I look at the heavens, the work of your fingers,
the moon and the stars which you set in place,

Lord, our Lord, how powerful is your Name
everywhere on earth.

What, then, is man, that you remember him,
the son of Adam, that he touches your heart.

Lord, our Lord, how powerful is your Name
everywhere on earth.

Yet you have made him almost a god,
and you have crowned him with glory and splendor.

Lord, our Lord, how powerful is your Name
everywhere on earth.

You make him lord of the work of your hands,
and you have laid the whole world at his feet.

Lord, our Lord, how powerful is your Name
everywhere on earth.

> *Then the baptist tries to say something*
> *briefly but well about*
> *(for example)*
> *being a baby,*
> *being born and baptized*
> *(preferably not about original sin*
> *and being lost),*
> *about Jesus, God,*
> *being a father and a mother,*
> *responsibility, love,*
> *having a future,*
> *being a person*
> *and so on.*
> *In this, he might perhaps*
> *read one of the following fragments:*

A FRAGMENT FROM THE GOSPEL OF MARK

Once people brought their children to Jesus,
with the intention of letting him bless them.
But the disciples sent them back.
When Jesus saw this, he was indignant and said:
Let those children come to me
and do not prevent them,

for the kingdom of God belongs to those
who are as these children.
Truly, I say to you:
anyone who does not accept the kingdom of God
as a child
will certainly not enter it.
And he put his arms round them
and blessed them
and he laid his hands on them.

A FRAGMENT FROM THE WRITINGS OF GERARD KORNELIS VAN HET REVE

If I take it as my point of departure that the fulfillment of man's destiny is to love God, then all that still remains is the question as to what kind of love I ought to set as my ideal of love for God. The answer to this question must be—the most unselfish and the most unconditional love. Is that the love of children for their father? That love is far from disinterested. It is mixed with fear of punishment and of loss of security. Is it then the love that exists between partners in love? Certainly this kind of love may include great moments of real disinterestedness, but it is also mixed with elements that are not unconditional, such as a desire to increase one's self-esteem, to dominate and to satisfy one's passion. Is it then the love that exists between brothers, sisters, friends? This love too is partly directed towards one's own preservation and one's own interest. What love still remains? Only the love of parents for their child. This love—if it is genuine—asks for nothing and gives everything. So we must love God as our own Child.

With the help of the seven-armed candlestick,
the baptist might also perhaps
tell the following story.

THE SEVEN FLAMES

As everybody knows,
there are seven flames in the universe
and together they form
the air that we breathe
and the ground beneath our feet—
in a word, they comprise everything.
But there are also
seven flames in every person,
because every person is a little universe
and that is why there are
seven candles burning
on that candlestick.

The first flame is the flame of the sun,
which is the source and the watchman
of all things.
Every child is just a little bit
born of the sun
and protected by the sun.

The second flame is the flame of langauge.
People look for each other
with words of fire
and a tongue of fire that stammers
is better than a head full of brains
that is silent.

The third flame is the flame of passion,
which teaches you how to love
and holds your whole body so tightly
that you become a burning soul,
a blazing tree that is not consumed.

The fourth flame is hunger and thirst.
It is written:
hunger is a fire that swallows stones,
thirst is a fire
that no sea can put out.

The fifth flame is God,
who sends out his sparks
into everything that lives,
up to heaven and down into the pit.

The sixth flame is the flame of music.
You can have this flame in your ears
to listen with others,
in your mouth, to sing with others,
in your hands, to play with others
and in your feet, to dance with others.

The seventh flame is the flame of hope,
which makes people into
children, wanderers and prophets
and makes them sing:
seventy times seven trees
will flower where we live,
light will stream upon the water.

I hope that your child
will become a person
from whom flames shoot out
and sparks fly.

> *If people feel like singing, another psalm*
> *can be sung now, or a song or this*

A SONG ABOUT PEOPLE

The birds can never live
    as men and women live.
They shelter in the trees
and find refuge in their song.
They sow no seed, but dream
and their future is but death.
We people cannot live
    as water flows along—
so rapid and so fleeting
and never feeling thirst.
The water goes on flowing,
but people are not so.

The walls are not so old
    as men and women are.
They crack with age, but sorrow
is quite unknown to them.
We people have to labor,
but bricks and stones do not.

We people do not fall
        as trees when they are old.
We have our sons and daughters—
a future human life.
The trees must fall and die,
but perhaps we people live.

> *Then we do something*
> *with questions and answers,*
> *words and water,*
> *a prayer, a gesture.*

THE NAMING OF THE CHILD

> *The baptist addresses the parents:*

By what name do you wish
your child to be called
now and in eternal life?

> *The parents name their child.*
> *The baptist repeats this name and says:*

May this name be written for ever
in the book of life,
in the palm of God's hand.

THE BAPTISMAL PRAYER

Lord God, our Father,
you have given your Son, Jesus Christ, to us

as the good shepherd
who knows us all by name.
We thank you
for your grace and your faithfulness,
for the new life that you have created,
for this child who has been born among us
and whom you have entrusted to us.
You have given him (her) ears to hear with
and eyes to see with.
Bless too this child's mouth,
so that he (she) may learn how to laugh
and to speak the language of men.
Bless also his (her) hands and feet
and may he (she) learn
from his (her) own experience
that everything that you have made
is good.
We ask you to shelter this child
and keep him (her) safe in this rough world.
Keep everything that is bad and inhuman away from him (her),
protect him (her) from evil influences
and never let him (her) be perverted.
May he (she) be secure with his (her) parents
and may we who are mature and responsible
never give scandal to this child,
but lead him (her) to the truth.
If, however, sin should ever have power over him (her),
be merciful to him (her), Lord God—
you make good all human guilt and shortcomings
and are yourself, even before this child is able to sin,
the forgiveness of all sins,
through Jesus Christ, our Lord.
Amen.

THE QUESTIONS

The baptist asks the parents:

Do you promise
to be a good father and a loving mother
to your child?

They reply:

Yes, we do.

Do you also promise
to bring your child up
in the spirit of the gospel?

Yes, we do.

Do you also promise
to remain faithful to your child,
whatever the future may bring,
and to respect him (her),
wherever he (she) may go,
and to remember always
that your child is born of God?

Yes, we do.

Part with your child, then,
and give him (her) to these two,
who will hold him (her) now
while he (she) is baptized
and who, in that gesture, promise you
that they will always
stand by this child in friendship.

THE BAPTISM

The parents give the child
to the godfather and godmother.
The children who are present
now come forward with their candles burning
and stand around the baptist
and the child who is to be baptized.

The baptist names the child
and says:

I baptize you
in the name of the Father,
the Son and the Holy Spirit.

The children lift up their candles
and call out: hurray!

The baptist anoints the child
and says:

I lay on you
the name of Jesus Christ,
I anoint you with his Spirit,
I sign you with his cross,
so that you may be filled
with the power and the disposition
that was in him, child of God,
today and for ever and ever.

He then says to the parents:

Receive this child,
embrace him (her) with love,

keep these words in your hearts
and be happy with each other.

> *The father receives the child back*
> *from the godmother*
> *and kisses him (her).*
> *He gives him (her) to the mother*
> *and she kisses him (her).*
>
> *In conclusion,*
> *something truly rousing is sung.*

Three Texts for a Wedding Day

For a marriage
solemnized and celebrated
with singing
in a house—
a church, for example.

A story
a song
a prayer.

THE STORY OF THE CREATION
OF MAN AND WOMAN

Incantation,
an introduction
that must be sung
broadly and lyrically
by several voices
and accompanied
by an organ or a harp,
violins and flutes.

Earth had been made,
but was desert,
still empty and hidden,
ways, tracks and mountains were there,
but no feet there to tread them,
seas there, but nobody there who might
walk on the waters.

There was no coming and going,
no looking, no trees there
or brushes, no leaves and no branches,
no flowers,
no water—

earth, fields and all birds
were parched and dry
and the sun
fell like a knife in the night
and closed in behind
the blind door of loving,
there mouths were thirsting
for no one.

There was the vault of the sky,
but no height and no hands there,
clouds were there and the fire
like a grey mist around things,
but still no stream like a voice
and no millstones that grind
and still no man who would open his lips
and hungrily eat,
who like a house on the bank of the river
is waiting.

Then, when the world was existing,
but bare and deserted:

> *Here follows a fragment*
> *from the book of Genesis*
> *to be read*
> *by a woman.*

Then God fashioned man
from the dust of the earth
and breathed into his nostrils
the breath of life.
In this way man became a living being.

Then God planted a park in Eden
in the east
and there he brought the man
he had fashioned.

He caused to spring up from the earth
every kind of tree, God,
beautiful to look at
and good to eat,
and in the middle of the park
stood the tree of life
and the tree of the knowledge of good and evil.

Then God said:
it is not good
for the man to be alone.
I will make him a helpmate
who is suitable for him
and who will give him an answer.

And God fashioned
from the dust of the earth
all the animals of the field
and all the birds of the sky
and led them to the man
to see what he would call them.
And whatever name the man gave
to everything that lived,
that name it would have.

The man gave names to all the animals,
to the birds in the air
and the beasts in the field,
but for the man there was no helpmate
who was suitable for him
and who gave him an answer.

Then God made the man fall
into a deep sleep
and he took one of his ribs away
and closed the hole with flesh.
Then God built the rib
that he had taken from the man
into a woman
and led her to the man.

Then the man said:
she is the one at last,
bone from my bones
and flesh from my flesh!
Woman will be her name,
for she is taken from the man.

That is why the man
leaves his father and mother
and clings to his wife,
and they become one body.

Now both of them were naked,
the man and his wife,
but they were not ashamed.

THE SONG OF THE BELOVED

I rose up from my bed at night
and went through all the city.
The God I love has gone away—
O my dear Lord, have pity.

I looked in all the streets and squares,
I thought I was behind him.
He gave no answer when I called—
I sought, but did not find him.

The watchmen came upon me there—
they wounded me and beat me.
O earth, have you seen him I love?
I long for him to meet me.

I wept for him who is my God,
until he came and found me.
I took him to my mother's house,
where his love might surround me.

Do not arouse your love too soon—
its call will always bind you,
no water ever puts it out,
its fire will scorch and blind you.

A TABLE PRAYER

For the celebration
of the Eucharist.
If possible it is to be sung
antiphonally,
by the leader, the choir
and all present.

May peace be yours and peace be yours.
May all that is good and makes for happiness
come upon both of you.
May peace be with you all
and in the whole world.

If you, there in your inaccessible light,
you who are God,
if you see and hear us here,
if we exist for you,
accept then our words of thanksgiving,
this song of great surprise,
on this day which you have made.

We who are simply people
and whose lives are short
have never seen you,
but we venture to sing your name

and in the words of people
we call you, with the names of centuries
we look for you,
O eternal, living God.

You said, "Let there be light,"
and the light was born;
you saw that it was good,
the land of the morning,
earth and heaven
and all the vaults of water and fire;
you saw that the trees were good
and all the beasts very good
and all the birds perfect;
then you said, "O man,"
and man was born;
but you saw man
and that he was lonely
and could not be comforted,
and so created him man and woman;
you changed and directed all paths
so that these two might find each other—
we thank you, God,
for having done it like this
and in no other way.

I ask you, God, complete them and bless them,
make them become more and more human
and let them experience in their bodies
that they are called
to be as good as God to each other,
that they may become more and more
like him who is your image, your Son,

Jesus of Nazareth, the new man;
he has shown us what life is,
what love does,
becoming a man for others
and giving himself, heart and soul,
to this world.

For, on the evening before his suffering and death,
as a sign of the spirit which filled him,
he took bread in his hands and broke it
and gave it to his friends with these words:
take and eat, my body for you.
Do this in memory of me.

He also took the cup with the words:
this is the cup of the new covenant,
my blood, shed for you
for the forgiveness of your sins.
Do this in memory of me.

O God, who are greater than all sin, all death,
and who made the son of men rise again,
you will also never let these two be lost.

Let nothing in them be lost,
because of today.
Keep them alive and let death,
which separates and makes everything dark and empty,
never come upon them.
Let them never tire of each other,
so that they may not falter,
for this world passes,
but love does not pass—
it is like the sea,
flashing like fire and stronger than death.

Keep them together in love,
write their names in the palm of you hand,
write them in your heart,
because of their friends, ourselves,
because of your son, the son of men,
who lives with you
now and for ever.

We ask you this, God, and with the words
which Jesus has given us
we come to you and sing "Our Father."

Our Father, who art in heaven,
hallowed be thy name.
Thy kingdom come.
Thy will be done,
on earth, as it is in heaven.
Give us this day our daily bread,
and forgive us our trespasses,
as we forgive those who trespass against us,
and lead us not into temptation,
but deliver us from evil.

Receive this bread
and share it with each other
and drink from this cup;
and know that he will be your God
for ever.

A Liturgy for a Dead Person

The one who is to lead in worship
and the dead person's friends
carry the coffin
to the front of the church.
The choir sings,
in dialogue with the people:

AN ANTIPHON FROM PSALM 90

You make people
crumble into dust,
you say: It is all over—
ah! children of Adam.

You have been a safe place to live in,
for us, O Lord, throughout all generations.
Within living memory you are God.

You say: It is all over—
ah! children of Adam.

In your sight, a thousand years
are like yesterday, a day that has passed.
You sweep us out like a dream in the morning.

You make people
crumble into dust.

The life of a man lasts seventy years,
or eighty, if we are strong.
Most of that is hardship and sorrow—
all at once it is over and we are gone.

You make people
crumble into dust,
you say: It is all over—
ah! children of Adam.

PRAYER

Said by the one who leads the worship
and answered verse by verse
by the people,
who sing,
"Lord, have mercy on us."

It is good
that you have come here
to say good-bye to this person
and to send him (her) on his (her) way.
I ask all of you
to pray with me:

Lord God, have mercy on him (her)
and on all of us.

Let us pray
to him who wants to be our God
and who did not shun our death
that he will know us
by our names
and that he will take us
into his peace.

Let us pray
that he will speak to us
in these words
here and now.
O God, you said,
"I will be there."
Do what you have promised.

Do not deny the work of your hands,
this person, whom you have made.
We cannot believe
that all he (she) meant to other people
is lost now, over and done with.
But we share the faith
by which he (she) held on to you
to the very end
to you, his (her) God and ours,
to you living for us
today and every day
for ever and ever.
Amen.

A READING FROM THE BOOK OF JOB

Man, born of a woman,
lives a short life that is full of sorrow.
Like a flower he blooms and withers;
like a shadow he flees away and is not lasting.
And is it towards such a one
that you turn your eyes, God,
is it such a one that you call before you
to be judged?

Was a clean man ever born of an unclean man?
No, there never has been one.
But if it is a fact that man's days are counted,
that the number of his months is determined by you
and that you have set limits for him
which he cannot pass,
then do not turn your eyes away from him
and leave him alone
until, like a hired man,
his work is finished.

Yes, there is still hope for a tree,
if it is cut down,
that it will go on living
and that its shoots will continue to sprout.
Even though its roots are dried up in the ground
and its stump is withered in the soil,
it will put out buds as soon as it smells water
and flower like a young plant.

But if a man dies, he remains lifeless.
If he breathes his last, where is he?

Like the water flowing out of the sea,
like a river running empty and dry,
man lies down and never gets up again.
He will not wake up out of his sleep.

If only you would hide me deep in the earth
and conceal me until your anger has passed!
If only you would set a fixed time
when you would think of me!
Can a man, once he is dead, live again?
If so, I would go on hoping
all the days of my hard service,
hoping until I was relieved.

AN ANTIPHON FROM PSALM 22

God, my God,
why have you abandoned me?

"My God," I call all day—you are silent,
I call through the night, and you just let me call.

God, my God,
why have you abandoned me?

Our fathers put all their trust in you,
they trusted and you have been their rescue.

God, my God,
why have you abandoned me?

But I am no longer a man but a worm,
scorned by men, despised by my neighbors.

God, my God,
why have you abandoned me?

Was it not you who drew me from the womb
and made me rest at the breast of my mother?
At birth I was put in the hollow of your hands,
you are my God from my mother's womb onward.

God, my God,
why have you abandoned me?

THE GOSPEL OF JESUS CHRIST ACCORDING TO JOHN

At that time, Martha said to Jesus:
Lord, if you had been here,
my brother would not have died,
but even now I know
that God will grant you everything that you ask him.
Jesus said to her:
your brother will rise again.
Martha replied:
I know that he will rise again
at the resurrection on the last day.
Jesus said to her:
I am the resurrection and the life.
Anyone who believes in me will live,
even though he dies.
Whoever lives in faith in me
will not die in eternity.
Do you believe this?

She replied to him:
I believe that you are the Messiah,
the son of the living God
who is to come into this world.

> *The dead person is remembered*
> *and honored*
> *in a short address*
> *and the bidding prayers*
> *that follow it.*
> *Then the choir and people sing:*

THE SONG "THE LORD HAS SEEN ME"

The Lord has seen me and to my surprise
he gave my heart new life, my eyes new sight.
I was reborn and came to life again
and in the dark he kindled a new light.
For he accepts my weakness as it is
and overcomes me with his silent might.
The Lord our God knows every one of us
and he has written our names in his hand.
He wants to live in us as in his house,
to plant his life in us as in his land,
to play with us and take us as his bride
and what we are he has already planned.
You visit us, your loved ones, in our dreams
and while we're sleeping sow your name like seed.
Just like the rain that falls upon the earth
or like the wind, you come in word and deed.
You seek us out and make us live again
and open to receive all that we need.

After the intermission,
the one who is leading the service says:
"The service of the table will begin now.
Let us pray."
There follows:

THE TABLE PRAYER

We name you, Lord our God,
and we bless you now
on this day which you have given us.
We adore you,
overwhelmed or serene,
alienated or rebellious,
believing and not believing
at the same time.
You are a God of living people.
You were not ashamed to be our God,
eternal and faithful
in life and death,
in good times and in bad.
Surely, then, you would not go back
on your promise, your name,
and not show mercy to this dead person?

We ask you this
for the sake of Jesus Christ,
our brother, your beloved Son.
You called him and sent him
to go ahead of us to you.
He became man
and was tested in joy and suffering,
but clung to you.

He fulfilled everything that is human—
our life and death,
giving himself, heart and soul,
to this world.

For, on the night that he was delivered up,
he took bread into his hands
and raising his eyes to you,
God, his almighty Father,
he gave thanks
and broke the bread
and gave it to his friends
with the words:
Take and eat,
this is my body for you.
Do this in memory of me.

He also took the cup
and, giving thanks to you, said:
This cup is the new covenant in my blood
shed for you and for all mankind
so that sins may be forgiven.
Every time you drink this cup,
you will do it in memory of me.

So whenever we eat of this bread
and drink from this cup,
we proclaim the death of the Lord
until he comes.

Therefore, Lord our God,
we present this sign of our faith
and therefore we call to mind
the suffering of your Son.

We remember
that he was crucified and buried,
but above all we remember
that you saved him
from death, that abyss,
and that he became for us
a name above all other names,
a man of peace,
living with you
and praying for us,
a man who will come
to make all things new.
Then there will be no more sorrow
and no more death.
Then he will call all of us,
the living and the dead,
by our names
on the day that you have appointed.

We ask you, Lord our God,
give us all the power of his life,
your Holy Spirit,
so that we may,
with hope and resolution,
continue on the way of life
and hold on to each other,
taking care that not one of your people
is lost.
Through Jesus and with him and in him,
may we find you
and, near to you,
those who have gone ahead of us.
May we see you
and speak with you, God,

as one person speaks with another.
We ask and implore you
to grant us this
now and for ever.
Amen.

Let us pray
to God our Father
with the words
that Jesus has given us:
Our Father, who art in heaven,
hallowed be thy name.
Thy kingdom come.
Thy will be done,
on earth as it is in heaven.
Give us this day our daily bread,
and forgive us our trespasses,
as we forgive those who trespass against us,
and lead us not into temptation,
but deliver us from evil.
Amen.

The one who is leading the service
lifts up the plate containing the bread
and the cup with the wine
and says:

This is the bread of the resurrection.
This is the cup of God's faithfulness.
Take, eat and drink,
and may peace be with all of you.

The bread is broken and shared
and the cup is handed round.
There follows:

THE SONG OF MAN ON EARTH*

To be a human being
is once for all be born on earth,
is all your life the pain of birth.
To be a human being
is living on the wind.

The trees all have their roots, yes,
they stand there firmly years on end,
but man's life leads around the bend.
The trees all have their roots, but
a man must pass along.

The foxes have their holes, but
mankind knows neither stand nor stay,
man's home is always down the way.
The foxes have their holes, but
will someone be our way?

People have many sorrows,
their bread and body cost them dear,
and we cause others pain and tears.
Who knows what comes tomorrow—
we wait for death so long!

To be a human being
is pain and blessing all at once;
is: search but not find all one wants;
is: resting in the earth when
our lives have run their course.

* This English version is by Forrest Ingram, S.J.

How shall we bring completion
to tasks that last for centuries—
a man whose life must one day cease?
Still we burn on with longing
till all things are fulfilled.

> *The one who is leading the service*
> *now stands at the end of the coffin*
> *facing the people*
> *and says:*

THE ABSOLUTION

We are gathered together here
around this dead body,
all that is left to us of this man (woman),
to pay our last respects to him (her)
and to do justice to his (her) life and death.
Keeping our eyes fixed
on the cross of Jesus Christ,
we say in groping faith
that this is not the end,
that our God is a God of the living.

Rather than his (her) body
we are left with the name of this man (woman),
which we speak now
with reverence and affection
and we pray:
Lord God, remember this name

which he (she) was given by other people
and by which he (she) is known
even though he (she) is dead,
the name that you have written
on the palm of your hand.
As a sign of our hope
that God will give a new and immortal body
to this man (woman) and to all of us,
and to bear witness
to our faith in the resurrection,
I bless this dead body
in the name of the Father and of the Son
and of the Holy Spirit.

> *The body is blessed*
> *with water.*

Let us now go in peace
and take him (her), whom we have had among us
during this past hour
for the last time, to his (her) grave.
We let him (her) go
out of our keeping
and place him (her)
in the earth, in the care of the living God,
in the name of the Father and of the Son
and of the Holy Spirit.

> *Flowers are placed*
> *on the coffin.*

May our prayers accompany him (her).

The coffin is taken out.
This song is sung:

No one lives for himself,
no one dies for himself.
We live and die
for God our Lord
and we are the Lord's.

Heaven

The heaven is the Lord's own heaven,
he has given the earth to men.
Psalm 115

No one knows anything about it any more. The very word
is irritating. What does heaven mean to us now? More or
less the same as illusion, fairy tale, escape, flight from the
world. Karl Marx, who was born a hundred and fifty years
ago, undoubtedly did something to all Christians when he
suggested that their religion—and indeed every religion—di-
verted the very heart of man, his energy and his commitment
away from this earth and allowed him to become lost in an
expectation of heaven, a hereafter.

The word "heaven" does, however, have at least one merit
—it still raises questions in our minds, makes us uncertain,
stimulates reflection.

Where is heaven? What is heaven? "Our Father, who art
in heaven." What does that mean?

To begin with, heaven is a vault, a firmament to which the
stars are fixed, and having floodgates through which the rain
falls. This at least was the primitive idea of heaven, what

people thought, for example, four thousand years ago. And we still feel the same way about it when, on a clear night, we search the heavens for the morning star, Venus, or for Castor and Pollux, the twins. Heaven is naked, clear, overcast. A man can move heaven and earth to obtain something. Marriages are arranged in heaven and we call heaven to witness if we are absolutely sure that we are right. Sometimes, although not so very often, we are in the seventh heaven, in the clouds.

"Heaven" is an upwards movement, a movement towards what is above us. It is a word for what is above us, in the sense of going beyond our understanding, and that is the most we can say in this sublunary existence. For example, another person is above us, as he is in himself, concealed and inviolable. You can photograph him, touch him, weigh him and operate on him. You can even plant someone else's heart in him. You can guess what is going on inside him, but you can never possess him. You can see him, look at him, but you cannot be him. "That I must see you and cannot be you, separated from you by my own eyes"—these lines of the poetess Vasalis evoke for me what another person is, another man in his distance, another man in his "heaven." Above and beyond my reach. You have always to go up to another person. It is really above and beyond you. In love or friendship or in any intimate relationship whatever, you just know this. Another person lives "in clouds and darkness" or, to express it in a different way, in "inaccessible light." And this is exactly what is said of God in the Bible, in the psalms and in testimony.

What is most above and beyond people is death. There has never been any word, either said or written, which exorcises death and there will probably never be any man who will be able to cope with death. "O death, O grasping, gluttonous thief, why have you never spared us, not even once?" The Russian writer Isaac Babel ends one of his stories with these words, found on a tombstone.

In his thoughts and in his longing and hope, man extends and perpetuates his life beyond death and sometimes explains death away in a poetic and beautiful conception of life after death. He cannot stop doing it, apparently.

All religions formulate a plan of a hereafter. The ancient Egyptian civilization, for example, bears witness to a grandiose expectation of life after death, seeking the kingdom of the dead above. The sun god took the dead in his ship to heaven, where the fields of a heavenly Egypt were spread out among the stars, fields in which the corn grew much more luxuriantly than it did on the banks of the Nile. In a ritual that was regulated down to the smallest details, every attempt was made to ensure that the dead would have a safe crossing to that heaven. Translated into the norms that still prevail in some parts of our own society, this means that, in ancient Egypt, many masses were offered for the souls of the faithful departed.

When Israel came away from Egypt (away from a strange and gabbling people, Psalm 114 tells us), she finished with these expectations of a life after death, with these illusions. For other people of Israel it was an exodus from a world of religious dreams and speculations about heaven. Henceforward, they were to be concerned with a radical task on this earth—that of becoming a nation, inhabiting a country, founding a city and doing justice to each other and all men, no more and no less than this. In doing this, their vocation was to have no other certainty, no other hope than simply the name of God. No image of him, nothing to hold on to, only the name, the sound of which died away with every voice that spoke it—Yahweh God, which means "I will be there for you." This means: you will see, only wait, do not grumble, live as best as you can, live here and now, inhabit this earth.

In the course of their hard history, at their best moments and in their greatest seers and prophets, the people of Israel experienced it as a tremendous relief that they no longer needed to direct their energy and their hope towards a life after death that could be represented in detail, but could turn this energy and longing to a God who could not be represented or imagined, a God who is now, a God with whom you can go forward, in questions and doubts of course, but also in mutual friendship, in not seeing and yet in seeing, in clouds and darkness, as it is said in the words of Psalm 97.

In Israel, believing is knowing what to expect. You do not expect a heaven, a hereafter—you expect God. And he is so near and yet far, just as people are near to and yet far from each other. The profundity and the grimness and the paradox of this faith in God has been expressed in a saying about the founder of Hassidism, the Jewish spiritual movement which revived and gave new life to the best of Israel's inspiration in the ghettos of Eastern Europe, a little story about the Rabbi Israel Ben Eliezer: "Once he was so dispirited that it seemed to him that he would never be able to share in the world to come. Then he said to himself: If I love God, what need have I of any world to come?"

Every man who is called to faith is himself Israel. He is called away from the Egypt of his speculations about heaven and invited to follow in the wake of "If I love God, what need have I of any world to come?"

That being with God which people sometimes experience here on earth in a memory, in a suspicion, in the testimony of someone else or in some other way, that being with God —can it ever cease? There have been people, in Israel and in the wake of Israel up to the present day, who have said it will not cease. People who have loved someone else until death also say sometimes that it will not cease. Perhaps, overcome by loneliness, they say those impossible words—what existed between us will never pass. And what do we say then, we who are near and see it and are outside it? Do we say: What nonsense, this is a flight from reality?

There are also people who dare to say: What I have with God will never pass. Or they say: That dead person, the one I loved who is now dead, has disappeared into God, is concealed in God. In the Bible, that is said of Moses and Elijah and Jesus of Nazareth, that they entered heaven, that they disappeared into God, that they were concealed in him. "In peace" is what we find on the earliest Christian graves, or "Live in God."

Heaven is a pseudonym for God. Heaven is this: God will be there for you. Words that are almost empty—no picture, no representation is involved in them. But sometimes, even if it is given to us for a moment and then never again, we hear and recognize in those words that God fulfilled his name in people. And when we say that Jesus of Nazareth was taken up into heaven, then what we are doing is saying falteringly that the least among men was saved in God and that our assailed and belittled existence as people will also be saved in God—I will be there for you.

The Book of Revelation, speaking about the last things and looking for images and likenesses to describe the name of God, says, in words which fall over one another and can hardly be made to agree with each other and which really give you nothing to hold on to, that he will not erase our names (that is, everything that we are, everything that we possess) from the book of life, that he will set up our bodies like pillars in his house, that he will write his name all over us, his name which is "I will be there for you," and that he will give us a white stone on which a new name is written. "Man" is our name, this man. But what is a man? He is tremendous, puzzling and almost nothing at the same time. He is divided, a stranger to himself, riveted to his body and nailed to his origin and his shortcomings. A doubtful identity. A man is only half-known in his own name and soon forgotten. Will the life never come when I may at last be man in a new name? Yes, some time in heaven, in God—"I make all things new," he says, he shouts out, at the end of that mad Book of Revelation.

We cannot, of course, find our way out of this story. We cannot get any further than the constant repetition of one thing. We shall see. We are still alive. Like a man who tries to go on living when he has buried his dead and then just finds other people to whom he can still be good. And so he goes on, without being given an answer to his questions, doing what he finds has to be done and living as best he can, here and now. And he will see.